Lean & Agile Made Simple

Paula Beattie

Enjoyed this book? Visit the author's website at www.leanagileworld.com

First published in Great Britain in 2019
Copyright © Paula Beattie 2019
Paula Beattie asserts the moral right to be
identified as the author of this work.

This book is dedicated to my beloved father, Julian Michael Winch
1935 – 2019

Contents

Foreword

Do any of the following apply to your organisation?

- It feels too hard to get the work done
- There are too many issues to fix and too little time to fix them
- Teams feel they are not empowered to make the changes they need
- People are exhausted by change and tired of having change 'done to them'
- Communication is poor between teams
- The customer is lost amongst it all

My name is Paula Beattie and I am a Lean and Agile consultant. I've worked in every kind of operation from tiny factories to global organisations, and I've been training teams in Lean all across the world since 2004. I'm also a certified Agile Scrum Master and Agile Kanban practitioner. I have a degree in Aeronautical Engineering, which is why a number of my stories come from the aerospace sector.

From my experience, the above issues apply to every non-Lean organisation that I have ever worked with.

Lean and Agile, if implemented fully and collaboratively, will solve them. By collaboratively, I mean that the people who are impacted by the change need to be those who help design the change, with managers alongside them trusting and supporting them.

Here is what I believe:

- Work should be joyous
- We should all love coming to work
- We should be able to easily succeed at doing our work

Instead, we let amazing people, who have so much talent and could contribute so much to our organisation, struggle to operate at the top of their game. They get bogged down with all the stuff that gets in the way of creating real value. They are not empowered or listened to. They are blocked, and as a consequence struggle to achieve success. Often out of pure frustration, they leave. What a waste. Enabling your team to succeed is the most important goal for a leader.

After graduating, my first management job was running a stores for an aerospace galley manufacturer. There were 12 storemen in my team who had been poorly managed for years, so it took several months to build their trust. When I started at the company, stores had a stock accuracy of 55%. This meant that a part was almost as likely to be in the wrong location or of the wrong quantity than the right one! And the company ran a stock ordering system based on this data. It meant that I spent the first month of that job in daily meetings being shouted at by production team leaders who were facing shortages on an hourly basis.

In my third week, the airframe manager told me, 'My operators worked all night on a part and then at 4am they tried to paint it, and the paint tin on your shelf in stores was missing. I spent a fortune on overtime and we still missed a deadline with our customer because your stock was wrong!'

I looked him in the eye and said, 'We will never run out of paint again.'

Then I raced into stores and asked, 'Where do we keep the paint?'

My team showed me a small room, about 2m x 3m. I thought, Surely we can manage a cupboard! We spent the day stock taking, re-labelling the shelves, colour coding the tins by sell-by date, and writing a standard operating procedure for managing the stock. We never did run out of paint again.

In 6 months our stock accuracy was 95% and in 12 months it was 98%. We almost doubled the accuracy and yet there was not one big thing we did over that time; just lots and lots of small incremental improvements over the whole department. This is the Lean principle of continuously seeking perfection. Whenever a problem appeared, we would try to fix the underlying cause. And almost every day a storeman would come up with an improvement idea – sometimes it was just tidying a shelf. It didn't matter what it was, because each change meant we were a little bit better that day than the day before. Think of it, do it, same day. My job was to do whatever it took to support them, whether it was asking for more money for new shelving, or taking their turn on the hatch. Individually, each improvement was tiny, but the cumulative effect transformed the department. It also transformed the morale of the team.

It was *their* transformation, not mine.

The production managers and senior team were exceptionally skilled. But we did raise the game of a few when they realised that stores could no longer be blamed for each and every failure.

We built a customer service feel to stores, where the customer was the shopfloor operator. Every aspect of improvement was centred around our customer. I didn't realise it at the time, but throughout this entire year, we were practising Lean. We were reducing waste, and focusing on creating customer value. We lived and breathed continuous improvement. We knocked that list of issues out of the park.

And it started with a cupboard.

Remembering this has always helped me to stop feeling overwhelmed when faced with the sheer enormity of a challenge.

After several more years of working in manufacturing, I became a self-employed Lean consultant in 2004. When I started my business, I wrote 30 letters to local ops directors explaining how I could help them. I received only one reply, but it was from Simon Roberts, ops director of McLaren Racing Ltd. That led to some really interesting Lean assignments with McLaren. I also helped implement Lean within the NHS, and also the pharmaceutical, food, utility, banking, nuclear, social housing and transport sectors. One of the best teams I ever worked with was London Underground in 2012 to lead on their winter weather plan, which covered all lines and involved 7,500 employees. This entire plan was devised, tested and implemented by the team in only 55 days, and resulted in a big reduction in lost customer hours across the whole network – despite it being the coldest winter for 50 years.

I discovered Agile in 2014 when working as Organisation Effectiveness manager for NHS Improvement. A year earlier I had helped the IT team streamline their key processes. We were lucky enough to have an excellent Agile coach called Barnaby Golden and he helped us implement Agile working in IT.. That team was very special, because all 70 of them embraced the learning and supported each other through the change to becoming Lean and Agile.

It was in 2016 when I had left the world of IT and realised that I was still thinking in terms of Agile every time I helped drive Lean improvements, that I realised Agile complements Lean perfectly in *any* organisation. Agile within software development is actually very complex, so in this book I've pulled out just those concepts of Agile that I use with Lean. I've learned that if we use Lean to engage with people and challenge waste, and an Agile approach to manage the change, we can create an environment where people are able to continuously improve. And that's one of the most important changes you could ever make.

I called this book *Lean and Agile Made Simple* because I use everyday examples to help explain the principles. That's because of two things. One, I think it helps to get my point across. We won't all have the same work place, but we do all use washing machines and dryers. Two, because Lean and Agile apply beautifully and luminously to the everyday world around us.

Our whole lives could take a shot of Lean and Agile.

This book explains in very practical terms how you can start to use a Lean and Agile approach and why you should. I really hope you enjoy reading it.

Introduction

Imagine you are in a hospital. A Lean consultant will ask, 'How can I help teams eliminate wasteful steps so that clinicians have more time to provide patient care?'

A *Lean and Agile* consultant will do the same, but will also think about how to deliver the change faster and more responsively via Agile. This book will explain both Lean and Agile and show you how to combine them together.

Here's an example of how using both Lean and Agile gives the best results:

Imagine you are designing and building a new airport from scratch. If you just used Lean, you would be reducing passenger queue times and wasted movement, because Lean focuses on eliminating non-value-added activity for the customer. But you would take a long time to build the airport because you would use a typical project management approach. You would 'Lean' your project but only when every item on your project plan was finished would your airport be opened. Typically, this would take years. And only then would you understand if you got every detail right.

If you used both Lean and Agile, you would still use Lean to eliminate waste and focus on the customer. But instead of doing one big project plan and launching your airport at the end of it, you would use Agile Scrum principles to just build one runway, one passenger hub and one control tower. After all, once these features are up and running, you are able to start using and getting income for your airport. You would 'inspect and adapt' and apply the learning from any mistakes as you expanded. Your learning is done early on, not right at the end. And if a major airline goes into liquidation, you can pull the plug on expansion and still have a viable airport because you delivered it in continuous 'chunks' of value rather than in lots of part-finished builds.

In a nutshell, Agile is about creating customer value faster and responding to change.

So by combining Lean and Agile, you have an optimised airport. You have eliminated non-value-added activity for passengers, started earning income early on, are able to respond to a changing environment and the customer experience is great.

I begin this book by explaining the philosophy of Lean, and some key Lean tools and techniques that I find particularly useful when facilitating change. Then I explain Agile concepts. After that, I show you why Lean and Agile should be used together to optimise change. Finally, I explain the best way to sustain the improvements you have made.

This book is for anyone who is interested in Lean, interested in Agile, or just plain interested in enhancing their work place. You can use the techniques for full-scale transformational change, or just one small improvement. It's a short book because Lean is about delivering just what you need and no more. This doesn't stop you reading further about any subject you find particularly interesting.

The other reason for not going too deep is that the one thing I can't teach is experience. The only way you get experience is by applying the learning and having a go. There are no perfect solutions, and there will be plenty of scenarios that I don't quite cover in this book. But if you understand the principles, you can trust your instincts, and inspect and adapt your approach.

Becoming a Lean Organisation

The truth about Lean

Consider this question:

Why are organisations loaded with waste?

This is often the first thing I ask in a Lean workshop. I give around 15 minutes for the teams to complete a flipchart with their reasons. It gets them up on their feet early on! Here are three things that I've learned:

1. Very rarely does anyone ever ask what I mean by 'waste'

This is the first time I will have used the word; it might even be the first time they have heard it in this context, and yet people can still answer the question. That tells me that waste is instinctive. You *know* that it means the stuff that gets in the way of doing the real work. The stuff that annoys you, because you just want to come into work and do a good job. The stuff that over-complicates your work life until you feel like biting off your own arm. Okay, I'm exaggerating, but only a little, because wasteful activity causes real stress.

And since Lean is about eliminating waste, then it stands to reason that Lean is instinctive too. Lean is common sense, non-complex, and non-complicated. You are probably doing a lot of Lean things right now, or at least attempting to. If you're new at Lean, you maybe just didn't know that there was a term for it, that's all.

So if you ever get a Lean consultant who explains painstakingly that Lean is a really difficult concept, or tricky to understand, my advice is to get rid of him or her. Fast. Clever people who cannot simplify things will just add cost to your business. What every organisation needs are people who can take a simple thing and keep it simple.

2. The bullet points don't change

That's right, no matter what the size of organisation, or type of industry, 90% of the reasons teams come up with for why organisations are loaded with waste are the same from one company to the next. Operational people will have a number of points around poor processes. Strategic leaders will come up with something around lack of vision. But the vast majority of the answers are the same whatever company I am in.

And that tells me that every organisation wanting to be Lean is starting off with the same issues.

It's how they address those issues which sets them apart.

I once met with three companies in one week, all thinking about starting a Lean transformation, all three in the same industry. A year later, two of those companies were already on their third cycle of improvements. The third company? They asked me to come back in and explain to them again about Lean. Maybe it was a better time for change, they said. I came in and told them about the other two companies who hadn't hesitated, and were making big improvements. The bad news, I said, is that these are your direct competitors.

3. It's about people

When the 15 minutes are up, I ask the team to put a tick against any bullet points that are all about *people*. Within a few minutes, they have ticked about 90% of them.

Examples will include poor communication, silo working, resistance to change, lack of empowerment, unclear roles, poor behaviours, too many meetings, poor leadership, lack of training, lack of problem solving skills, poor involvement of those who *do* the work by those who make decisions *about* the work and so on.

This is important. Lean is often thought of purely as a way of removing waste from *processes*. But when you think about it, none of the causes of waste above will be eliminated by focusing on improving the process.

Current State　　　　　　　　　　　　　　　　**Desired Future
State**

Let's say that Current State is where your organisation is now, in terms of how Lean it is. Desired Future State is where you want to move it to, ie a Lean work place. If the only thing you plan to work on to move you from left to right are your processes, then your organisation will never be Lean. Those lovely new processes you designed with those nice representatives from each team? They won't work, because the *mindset of your people will still be in 'Current State'*.

And when you impose new processes on people without changing all of the people issues, the changes never succeed. Not in a deep, meaningful way. Consciously or subconsciously, people will apply current thinking to new processes, and the end result is a lot of effort, and not much change.

Lean organisations are courageous organisations, because they understand that real change, of the type that changes how people fundamentally *think,* takes strong, sustained leadership. Changing your organisation into a Lean one is hard. It is painful. If it were easy, and just about streamlining processes, almost every company in the world could become Lean in about 12 months.

The reason it takes between 3 – 5 years to truly transform an organisation into a Lean one is that change involves people. And people make it hard.

Interesting, but hard.

To truly become Lean, everyone in that company needs to understand Lean and be willing to apply it *all the time*. The best organisations arrange Lean training for *everyone,* not just a favoured few. And most importantly, they ensure that all the 'people' things are worked on as well, such as values, behaviours, culture, leadership styles, performance appraisals, meeting habits, HR policies, communication, and so on, so that everything is aligned with Lean. They start from the top. Managers are role models. The vision is not for a Lean organisation. The vision is for an organisation that gets Lean so well, it doesn't even need to use the term.

And please note that *nothing* kills Lean faster than when people are told the organisation is 'going Lean', but the senior team don't change. They still stick to the same old cumbersome policies, or continue to avoid challenging poor behaviours, or insist on sending out long boring emails that waste everyone's time. I once calculated that a director's 500-word email incurred 9 hours of a team's time to read (assuming they didn't just delete it) and showed him how it could have been written in just 37 words.

For a Lean organisation, you need Lean leadership. It is the single most important aspect of the change. Managers needs to walk the walk, not simply talk the talk. (Or as I say to my family on one of our hikes, 'Less yacking and more tracking.')

Make no mistake, Lean is not an initiative you can simply usher in the back door and hope it takes root. If you do, you will have *an* impact, but it will be a small incremental change, not a transformational change. There is a difference. A transformational change is a *big* change for your organisation. A very big change. By the time you have finished, everyone will see the world very differently.

So where did Lean come from? What is it really? And why would an organisation want to become Lean in the first place?

Where did Lean come from?

The philosophy of Lean (and it is really a philosophy more than anything else) is based upon the Toyota Production System of Japan.

To understand how the TPS developed, picture Japan at the end of the World War Two. As a country, it needed to dramatically rebuild its economy, and Japanese industrialists were charged with bringing the country – via its passenger car production companies – back on its feet again. These Japanese industrialists visited American factories, but it was the American supermarkets that really got them thinking.

'Why can't we create car factories that look like this? A place for everything and everything in its place. Systems that replenish stock when stock is consumed.'

So instead of using the conventional mass-production technology that they had seen in the American car plants, Toyota focused on developing their own in-house production system using this learning.

Ford and General Motors were massive heavyweights in the US automotive industry back then, and they were hugely subsidised by an American government keen to grow its own economy amidst the boom. Optimism was in the air, you could say. So if machines in their car plants were bottlenecks, they bought more machines. They had the capital to throw around.

In Japan, however, money was scarce. If machines became bottlenecks, Toyota couldn't just go out and buy another machine, so its people had to learn how to *remove* bottlenecks, and one of the best ways to do this, they discovered, was to reduce batch sizes. If you break down work into smaller batch sizes, you can move or flow the work faster through the process, because large batches *always* result in the work queueing or waiting to be worked on. And queuing is the *opposite* of flow.

But you can't run a batch of 10 items on a machine that takes a day to set up, that would be insane. This meant that the Japanese focused a huge amount of effort on reducing set up times for their machines, and this later led to the concept of SMED (Single Minute Exchange of Dies). The important point is that the Japanese exploited their key weakness (lack of investment) to become better at reducing batch sizes and increasing flow. Guess what? These techniques are perfect starting points for Lean.

Over the next three decades, Japanese gurus such as Taiichi Ohno would identify the key manufacturing principles that would become the foundation of Lean – creating customer value, making value flow, reducing waste such as inventory, and introducing the concept of pull, as seen in those supermarkets.

Womack and Jones in their 1990 seminal book, 'The Machine that Changed the World' perfectly explained the full power of Lean principles and how they could be applied to an entire organisation. For the first time, people realised that you didn't need to be an automotive company to apply Lean. This fired the imagination of CEOs everywhere. And the Lean journey took off in the Western world.

What is Lean?

The definition of Lean is very simple. **It is delivering value to your customer, as defined by your customer, whilst eliminating waste.**

(Notice that I say that the customer defines the value. In one high street bank I consulted for, there was a customer service person in every meeting. That person continuously analysed customer complaints and feedback and was able to present the customer's viewpoint in every decision and discussion. Hugely powerful stuff. It kept the Voice of the Customer permanently at the centre of the operation).

Waste is defined as anything that does not contribute to creating customer value. To me, it's even worse than that – it's the stuff that *gets in the way of creating value*, and a Lean organisation seeks to eliminate waste so that *more value can be created*.

For example, EasyJet created the concept of 'no frills' air travel. This is a *Lean* concept. EasyJet challenged whether all customers really valued tickets, travel agents, plastic-tasting food, allocated seat numbers, excessive baggage, free earphones and big expensive airports. What if some customers just wanted to pay to fly from A to B, safely and on time, for a lower cost, and were happy to book online flights themselves, have comfortable but basic non-reclining seats, and buy a sandwich on board if they wanted to? What would that mean?

Well, for EasyJet it meant that there was much less admin, no paperwork, no travel agency commission and quicker plane turnaround times. There were fewer aircraft ovens to heat up food, lighter seats and so costs were reduced around the aircraft design. And since there were no meals, they needed fewer airline staff to serve food, and interestingly, fewer toilets! Both of which resulted in more payload ie more passenger seats. There were also greatly reduced costs in airport charges from using smaller airports and having faster turnaround times.

And the customers? They were only paying for what they wanted, and EasyJet were able to pass on some of their cost savings to them so that the flights were cheaper. If they wanted extra features, they paid for the privilege, but the basic value-adds of on time, safe and cheap were the fundamental building blocks that EasyJet focused on delivering.

And all EasyJet had done was to understand and focus on what their customers really valued and then *design their entire operation such that it delivered just that value, and nothing else.* They saw everything else as waste, and eliminated it. Lean, in a nutshell.

It has of course become the standard way of air travel for the vast majority of us. EasyJet haven't always got things right, but their courage in being the first to challenge, take apart and rebuild the accepted status quo in one of the world's most competitive marketplaces is inspiring.

I have to add that I was once accused by an EasyJet cabin attendant of flushing my baby's nappy down the aircraft toilet, since it had become blocked soon after I had used it, and glowered at by Stelios himself as he stood behind her. Not a pleasant experience. If I hadn't had a 4 week old screaming baby in my arms, I would have explained that since I was a manager for the company that manufactured their toilets, there was probably no one on the plane less likely to flush a nappy down it than me. But hey, I was a woman with a baby, so she jumped to conclusions.

Truth be told, Stelios used that toilet just after me, so maybe it was him all along.

Delivering just value … and nothing else

Let's have another think about what this means.

Start by being careful of the word 'value'. Just because your customer tells you that the real value you create is X, doesn't mean that having 27 meetings about X is adding value to your operation.

A Lean organisation not only understands and focuses on delivering the value for its customers, it also ensures that it uses the *absolute minimum amount of effort to create that value.*

This means that its teams would have the minimum number of meetings necessary, generate the minimum amount of paperwork, send the shortest and fewest number of emails, have the lightest governance possible and wait the smallest amount of time between starting and finishing the process … basically they would expend the least amount of effort for the output required. Why? Because all the time they spend doing the above things, they could have been creating even more value!

Think about the worst company you ever worked for. It is possible that at least one of the following accounted for it having this dubious accolade: you spent far too much time in meetings and rarely found time to actually do any work; the work you did had to be constantly re-done because too many people reviewed it; you were forever waiting on someone to make a decision so nothing ever moved forwards; you felt like a lone voice in the wilderness shouting 'there's a better way!' without anyone ever hearing you; and actually doing the work was like rolling a boulder uphill with one arm tied behind your back and your ankles bound together. In other words, it reminds me of a lady that my mother once described to me: 'Nice person, but talking to her was like having an elephant sitting in your lap for 4 hours.' In other words, painful.

Here is what I truly believe: work should be exciting and rewarding. I have been lucky enough to work with incredible people, who are open to change, who are passionate about removing waste and who love to focus on delivering value. When you are lucky enough to have this as your work environment, with a boss who truly wants his or her team to succeed, you understand exactly why organisations need Lean. Who in their right mind *wants* to come to work and be prevented from creating value? No one. Well, okay, there may be one or two people, but the vast majority of people genuinely want to come to work and do their job well. As a manager, your single most important job is to facilitate this. It is *not* to performance manage them. It is *not* to ensure that *you* succeed. As a manager, your main job should be focused on giving your team a common purpose and supporting them in removing waste so that *they* can succeed. It's really that simple. Listen to their issues and empower them as much as possible to make improvements and organise the work themselves. Why get involved in every detail of the day to day? You can save your energy for the big changes. For the vision and strategy. Doesn't that sound like a good place to work?

So the real question is – why *wouldn't* an organisation want to be Lean?

Notes

The 5 Principles of Lean

Lean is a philosophy. It is a mindset, a way of thinking and looking at what is really going on, to *really see* the changes that need to take place if you are to transform your organisation into one that focuses all its efforts on delivering value to the customer. There are 5 key principles of Lean.

1. Define the value that your customer wants from your product or service

Remember the EasyJet example. They started by asking what the customer really wanted. Strip it back to basics. A publishing company said, 'Knowledge' when I asked them what value their customers were paying for. (And remember that knowledge has the power to transform lives). When I asked Rolls Royce managers what value their aircraft engines created, they simply replied, 'Thrust.' I would add the word 'Safe', but if the value-add of a highly complex product can be expressed in two words, so can yours.

2. Define the value stream

These are the process steps that create the value from start to finish. *They include all wasteful steps.* Start with a high level map of around 10 steps. Then break it down into more detail, including the backward flows ie when things go wrong. You need to map in enough detail to show the waste.

By the way, it's not unusual for me to map a key business process with the team and discover the process is 95% non-value-added, particularly in service organisations. Or that there are 20 steps needed before any value at all is created.

For example, think of passengers hiring a car at a foreign airport. A detailed process map for car hire could include customers having to find an official to ask for directions to the poorly signed rental office, walk across a burning hot carpark towards it, join a long queue, fill in lots of paperwork (why? The car was booked online – they knew you were coming! They had all the information!), avoid buying insurance for CDW (a scam, book it separately), walk miles to find their car, check for unrecorded damage, walk miles back again to report the damage, and spend 10 minutes working out how the weird key works in the ignition, or how to release the handbrake. Then finally drive off! This is the true value stream. Always map from the point of view of the customer. The hire car manager is probably super proud of their air-conditioned office, and doesn't realise that every time the queue builds up, people are waiting outside in the heat. Or that customers got stressed finding it, loaded up with prams and suitcases, as it wasn't clearly signed in the first place.

From the customer's viewpoint, the only value-added steps in the above process are 'drive off'. These are the only things that a customer is willing to pay for, other than offline activities such as cleaning, washing, maintaining and fuelling the car. The total number of process steps may well be over 50, when you include all the movement, paperwork and system input, none of which the customer cares about.

3. Make the value flow

Eliminate waste so you flow from value-added step to value-added step. Try to ensure that everything is Right First Time, so there are no backward loops involving rework. Reduce batch sizes, as we will see later.

4. Pull rather than push

Pull is all about delivering to the customer at the time that the customer wants your goods or service.

With manufacturing, it has a very specific meaning, where you only produce an item when the customer wants (ie pulls) it. The customer might be the end user, or they might simply be the next person down the production line. You build up a small, pre-agreed level of stock, but then if your customer isn't ready to pull from you, you stop working. This sounds counter-intuitive – surely if you're not working, you're not creating value! *But* it prevents you mindlessly creating inventory and pushing it around to the next person irrespective of whether they have capacity.

In its simplest terms, imagine eating food at Christmas. Most of us over-indulge – we eat even when we aren't hungry. That's push. Eating only when your stomach needs filling is pull!

Now imagine you are doing your Christmas food shop at the supermarket, and the checkout person is swiping your items at the till. This sends a signal to the food suppliers telling them their stocks on the shelves need replenishing. This is a pull system, as it pulls the stock from the supplier onto the shelf only when needed.

I once worked in a paint factory as Continuous Improvement manager. The tins for the paint would be sent by the supplier according to *their* manufacturing schedule, and our factory managers would take on the problem of hunting around for storage space, or expediting shortages. All of this was eliminated

> Understanding pull has many advantages in real life too. When my daughter was studying for A levels, she realised that in exams, she was simply *pushing* lots of information at each question in the hope that something would resonate with the examiner and she would get some marks. This wasn't working. Instead, she learnt to think about what value the question was *pulling* from her, and only give this information and no more. The examiner could quickly see the value in her answers, she didn't waste time on giving non-value-added information, and her marks soared.

when we worked together to change to pull – we only allowed delivery when we required the stock. Storage issues disappeared. And of course we stopped paying for stuff that we didn't yet need.

It works in non-manufacturing too. Organisations who use pull become very aware of what value their customers are after. You make a basic product at a competitive price, and then allow the customer to pull any additional features that they require. And pay for them. No-frills air travel from before is a good example. The customer has the choice of adding extras such as speedy boarding and extra baggage, without paying for anything they didn't want.

A while ago, I worked with a publisher of e-books, whose biggest gripe from their teams was the effort required to develop all the whizz-bang features that were offered with each e-book. I was interested in how they knew that their users really wanted these features. The answer? 'We don't actually know, we just assume they do.'

All of these new features meant that the teachers had to re-learn the e-book each academic year before they could teach it. Was all this really necessary? They sold to poorer countries, with much lower educational budgets. What if these customers just wanted a basic e-book that was cheap? If they wanted any extra features, they could pay a little extra for them. This would also generate intelligence as to which features were most wanted, leading to better product development.

Giving everything irrespective of when or whether it is required is a perfect example of push. What I was suggesting to the publishing house was a change to pull.

5. Continually seek perfection

This is the link between Lean and Continuous Improvement. I could never do an improvement without thinking in terms of Lean. Equally, I could never do a Lean project without encouraging the team to continually improve the outcome.

I remember developing a Lean training program with a manager, for him and his team. He asked me at the end of the meeting, 'What improvement can I expect from my team as a result of this training?'

I looked him in the eye and said, 'That's a good question. Here's a more important one. What can *they* expect from *you*?'

Everyone in an organisation should be prepared to continuously improve. Without exception.

Notes

Chapter Three

The 7 Wastes Plus 1

The Japanese believed that all waste could be categorised into seven different types – the 7 Wastes. Then the Western world pointed out that they had missed one – the Waste of Talent (also known as the Waste of Skills). Instead of calling these the 8 Wastes, which would have been too easy, we call them the 7 Wastes Plus 1.

By the way, one thing I always say to teams is that the aim is not for them to be able to recite the different types of waste. The aim is for them to develop a gut feel that something *is* waste, and why. If they can see waste, they can eliminate it.

Here they are:

1. The Waste of Waiting and Delays

The most insidious of all the wastes, because you just don't notice it. 5 minutes here, 5 minutes there … what's the difference, right? But did you know that 5 minutes every day spent doing something that adds no value amounts to 2.5 days per year? Which sounds deceptively low, until you stop and visualise *how many* 5 minutes per day you waste, and *how many* people in your company are wasting them. Then you realise the huge savings that can be unlocked by tackling this waste.

Ask your team – what is the biggest cause of delay? Is it waiting for work to arrive? Try using pull to avoid the feast and famine cycle. Is it waiting for decisions, or working out how to move forwards? Get standard processes in place for at least 80% of what they do. Is it waiting for a resource to become available? First check that the task adds value. If not, eliminate it. If it is needed, can it be automated in part? Can you reduce dependencies by upskilling other team members so they can do some or all of the work? For example, rather than waiting for my plumber to become available for half a day, can I remove the existing radiator and drain the system myself, so he can squeeze me into a 2 hour slot and fit my new one?

If an example of the Waste of Waiting in your organisation is people being repeatedly late for meetings, this is a disrespectful way to treat colleagues. Don't fall into the trap of accepting this behaviour.

The best way to counter this in your organisation is to have 10 minute meetings around a board. That's Lean. Then if they are late, they will have missed the entire meeting.

The silent killer of an organisation is the acceptance of mediocrity.

The Waste of Waiting is what I call 'Stop-Start'. It is a killer of momentum. Years ago I worked in the public sector where literally nothing could be done on a project without approval from the monthly directors' meeting. And when you looked at the decisions that were needed, the people on the ground were in a far better position to make them. I'm all for good governance, but only where it adds value. Waiting for a decision sapped all of the energy from that project and caused pointless delays.

2. The Waste of Over Production

This is producing more than you need to. What is the value that our customers want? We need to understand the value-add part of what we are doing or creating or building, and do the minimum amount of work necessary to achieve it. Any more than that is the Waste of Over Production. In this book I will try to explain Lean and Agile in the minimum number of pages possible. Why do more?

When I was a project manager in the aerospace industry, I discovered that the designers loved designing all the bells and whistles. Clever little details that they could demonstrate their superior design skills with. The problem was, someone needed to pay for these little extra features, and if the customer didn't want to pay, as a company why were we doing them? They were also the items that were most likely to cause delay to production, and as an aircraft interiors manufacturer, you don't miss delivery dates. Not unless you want to reimburse the daily cost to that airline of not being able to fly the plane.

When we don't continually check our bearings on the above question, we are in danger of going beyond the scope. People are very well meaning, and generally like to do more than they are asked to do, especially around features that they enjoy doing. But that doesn't mean that they are working on something that adds value. I realised our customers were always less impressed with snazzy features than the

The scene with Rowan Atkinson as a sales assistant in *Love Actually* demonstrates this waste perfectly as he insists on over-wrapping a gift. In the EasyJet example from Chapter 1, the Waste of Over Production was targeted, by ensuring they weren't delivering more than what their customers were prepared to pay for.

Why send out long emails? The fewer words you use, the less you will need to change when you review them before sending. People will typically only remember 10% of what you say, so why not just say the 10% that matters? This also applies to presentations. The majority of presentations are just lots of boring PowerPoint slides with text on them. I run 5 day workshops on Lean with about 10 slides in total – the rest of the time I use flipcharts and interaction to make it engaging. No one will remember the information on lots of slides – again, just show the 10% that matters and keep slides to an absolute minimum. Your audience will love you for it.

designers expected them to be, and always more annoyed when the basics didn't work!

Another way I see the Waste of Over Production is when a team works really hard on one part of the process, for it to just sit there waiting until the next team downstream is ready for it. This stop-start is hugely wasteful (and overlaps with the Waste of Waiting). It's the Waste of Over Production because the first team worked harder than they needed to, without creating any more value to the end customer. The best way to counter this waste is to change to pull instead of push.

Finally, beware of work that is done just to keep a team 'busy' or to justify its existence. Using a team to work on a project that will unblock another team is fine, but if that project is low priority then this is the Waste of Over Production. Stop tying up teams in low value work, and get them to help with the high value stuff, or use their time on improvement activities instead.

3. The Waste of Inventory

In manufacturing, inventory is either raw materials (work not yet started), work in progress (work that has been started but not yet completed), or finished work (completed but not yet shipped). It consists of physical parts, so it is easy to see and challenge.

Why reduce inventory?

Well, until that part has been shipped, it's not earning you money. It also costs labour to unload it, locate it, check it, provide heating and lighting, rent the space, manage it, pick it… When I was stores manager, I would insist that stores was not a dumping ground. It was a temporary housing place for parts that were on the move.

(Around the same time we purchased a house with a spare bedroom and bathroom on the top floor. My mother would somewhat ominously call it a 'granny flat.' I told her, 'It's not a granny flat. It's a temporary housing place for guests who are on the move!')

Think of your fridge at home. It is likely to contain items still unopened, items that have been part eaten, and so on. The more of these items you have in your fridge, the more likely you will be to miss a sell-by date and have to throw something away. The higher the inventory, the greater the waste. Shopping more frequently and in smaller quantities reduces the level of inventory, increases the turnover of food and is likely to save you money, even with the increased cost of fuel. In fact, those special offers encouraging you to buy in bulk are renowned for being one of the prime causes of food waste. I now have a small fridge, and I can see everything in there at a glance. When we had a huge fridge, the amount of food that got thrown out was ridiculous.

> **THE AGILE MANTRA**
>
> **Stop starting and start finishing.**
>
> Start challenging why you are taking on more work in your team, when you haven't yet delivered what is already there. Remember that the lower the level of work in progress (wip), the faster you will deliver to your customer. So try to finish the work before starting on any more. And always try to work in your customer's priority order.

Another example is your wardrobe. In the typical wardrobe you are unable to see the clothes that you really like, because of the vast stock of items that you no longer wear. How often have we all bought a new item of clothing, only to find something just like it hidden in our wardrobe or ironing basket that we had completely forgotten about? Clear out all those items that no longer add value to your life, so that you can use those items that *do*. And read the chapter on 5 S.

Often the biggest cause of the Waste of Inventory is having lots of work that has been started but not completed. In other words, work in progress, or wip. Work only has value to the customer once it is complete. No one wants a sofa or coffee table to be delivered without the legs.

High levels of wip mean you are tying up people, resources and systems to work on lots of things, without actually delivering to your customer. And the more wip you have, the more time your work is going to spend *waiting* to be worked on, rather than *being* worked on.

4. The Waste of Transport

In manufacturing, this waste is the unnecessary movement of parts around the shopfloor.

In offices it is about the movement of documents, emails and files, so it's harder to see. But think of the number of revisions of a document and the sign-offs required, and ask yourself – do these fundamentally add value? I once met a team who had worked for months on amending process documentation because it got reviewed by so many stakeholders, and moved backwards and forwards between them all with suggested changes. The team had to re-write it all immediately after Go Live because it still wasn't fit for purpose.

> When I was Continuous Improvement manager at a paint factory, the production managers were very proud of all their forklift trucks, because they simply didn't stop working during the day, moving the paint cans from the warehouses to the lines. As we had huge levels of stock, lots of cans had to be moved around to get to the ones they wanted. But in their minds, a busy factory was a productive factory. Actually, the reverse is usually true. The busier the factory, the greater the waste.
>
> It was difficult to convince the production managers that moving the paint around was wasteful. Waste is the hardest thing to challenge when it becomes part of the work.
>
> I finally had to tell them, 'No one is going to walk into B&Q and pay £19.99 for a can of 5 litre premium paint, and then dig in their pockets to give you another 50p because the paint had moved 57 times around the warehouse before it got to the store. Would *you* pay it?'

A Lean approach would have reduced the documentation that the team needed to produce in the first place and the amount of reviews required. Post launch, the process documents could have been finalised with any changes. This would have significantly reduced the Wastes of Over Production, Transport and Rework.

The brutal truth is that if a customer won't pay for it, why are you doing it? And all the time you are creating waste, what aren't you doing?

Adding more value.

5. The Waste of People Movement

In manufacturing, this is often linked with the Waste of Transport. In offices, it's sometimes about staff travelling unnecessarily to meetings (or a poor office layout). I once worked at a company that had two sites in London, and I estimate people spent 6 hours a week travelling to meetings. Once the sites merged, it was interesting how that travel time just got absorbed into everyday life. No one had an extra 6 hours free every week to think up more improvements!

One of the most common reasons for the Waste of People Movement is the effort required in accessing information. Movement is still waste if you're sitting at your desk. For example, poorly designed systems forcing you to use far too many screens. Systems that aren't integrated so you have to duplicate data entry into more than one system. A hospital I have helped have over 400 different systems or applications across 3 sites, and only a tiny percentage of them actually 'talk' to each other. So users need to duplicate data entry into multiple systems to get a full picture of the patient record and manage patient care.

The true cost of how much time these systems are causing expensive people to waste as they navigate, train staff, create Excel spreadsheets as work-arounds and maintain multiple applications is rarely factored into the financial decision-making around procurement.

Call centres bouncing customers around teams to answer a question is another example of this

> I once worked with a food testing company. They checked the cooking instructions for ready meals by cooking the food in a test environment and getting the public in to sample them. We persuaded the MD to do a typical walk from goods inwards to the kitchens, use the poorly laid out kitchens to make the food and then wheel everything to the sample rooms. It was the best way to get her to understand how painful the layout was. Then we proved that each person walked a minimum of 5 miles per week, around a small factory, just to carry out the process. She looked at me and said, 'Basically, I am paying people to walk food around my company.' She was right.

waste. In fact, the Waste of People Movement is probably the most frustrating of all wastes as you can never delude yourself that it is a good use of your time.

6. The Waste of Over Processing

While the Waste of Over Production is *producing more* than you need to, the Waste of Over Processing means making things *more complicated* than they need to be. From your customer's point of view, how many steps do they need to go through to consume your goods or service? (Also see Lean Consumption).

Walk into any supermarket for a drink and a sandwich–they won't make you walk around the store. In general, you won't need to walk more than 100 steps from start to finish. (This of course also reduces the Waste of People Movement). There will be a separate kiosk, just inside the entrance, with everything it needs to serve you quickly. If a customer wants a simple thing, deliver it quickly. Fast track it and make it flow. Everyone needs a fast track process for a simpler customer journey.

In hospitals, using day surgery units instead of main theatres for minor operations is another example of reducing the Waste of Over Processing, as are ambulatory care teams to help A&E patients who can be treated in a chair rather than a bed in a ward. All these activities take pressure off the main queues by creating a fast track process.

Ask yourself, Have we too many check points? Is the governance at the right level? Are there simply too many steps to get the job out the door? Try to simplify the

> It is not unusual for me to map a process and fill a wall with the steps required. The team are then at pains to explain that they do, after all, deliver a highly complex product at the end of it.
>
> So I ask, 'What is the *cheapest* part that goes through this process? How much does it sell for?'
>
> Often, it's about £10! That's right: £200 worth of admin incurred for a £10 sale. They are better off giving the customer £10 and declining the order.

process (in the next chapter we will look at SECAR which is an excellent framework to do this).

Trying to eliminate this waste is one of the most powerful improvements you can make. And you will always improve your customer service levels as you do so, because customers feel the pain of over-complicated

7. The Waste of Rework and Defects

Rework is everything you have to do because your process hasn't enabled you to achieve Right First Time. A key cause is defects, which is why the two are lumped together with this waste. I remember one guy fixing a defect on an aircraft galley, and saying to me, 'Good thing we get paid for this.' I told him he was wrong. We got paid once, to do it right. The single most important thing to remember about this waste is that **you can only add value once.**

I once worked with a manufacturing team who said to me, 'It's funny. We never have time to do it right, but we always have time to make it twice!'

My father was a terminally ill patient with acute leukaemia, and my mother had support in caring for him at home from district nurses, NHS healthcare community services, a quick-response team, a hospice and specialist nurses. For 3 days following his death, every community service arrived at her door asking how he was doing and prepared to help look after him. Some of them came more than once! Clearly there was no system in place to ensure that his death had been communicated to those involved in his care. Each nurse and healthcare assistant felt acute embarrassment when given the news by my mother, who was shocked at having to repeat herself and be continually disturbed during the worst week of her life. There was a serious defect in the process.

Another example of defects that I regularly see in the NHS is where the process is reliant upon a patient ringing to say that they haven't received their appointment for the next step. In other words, the patient is the check and balance! This is a *broken process*. It is also unsafe.

Process mapping is excellent for identifying defects and rework loops. I have often witnessed one person saying, 'I do this step because I know it saves you time!' only for the next person down the line to exclaim, 'I never know why you do that bit! It takes me ages to unpick it every time!'

And often these people sit no more than 10 feet away from each other. They just never have conversations around waste.

Two tips when trying to tackle this waste:

i. Look where rework occurs late in the process

Although all rework is bad, rework that occurs right at the end of a process is the worst of all, as the backward loop is the longest. All those pairs of hands now have to do the work again. And all that time, they could have been creating value.

ii. Look where bottleneck resources are made to do rework

By definition, a bottleneck does not have sufficient capacity to meet demand, and will therefore limit the rate of output of your process. So stop your bottleneck resources wasting precious time on rework. Fiona is an overworked copy editor. Imagine her editing a book that was later found to be poorly researched and ended up having to be rewritten for a different market. She has to edit it all over again! You should relocate the step where market research confirms the book is 'Go' *before* the editing step, so that Fiona only gets to work on books that have already been green-lighted. This also forces the right questions to be asked early on.

Of course, the key is to try to prevent the failure in the first place. Is it possible to get something Right First Time, In Full, Every Time? See Quality Assurance and Poka Yoke.

Note that the Waste of Rework will often generate many other types of waste.

The key to eliminating this waste is to understand what is preventing Right First Time. When mapping a process, people always tell you about what *should* happen. It's what I call The Sunny Day route. You need to find out where the process fails (the Rainy Day route) and how often. It often involves moving backwards through the process, as steps have to be repeated. Value should always flow from left to right in a process map, so a backward loop is usually a sign of the Waste of Rework and Defects. Why is the work having to go back to someone? It's usually because there's a defect, or because they don't have all the information they need at the right point. Make the rework visible, particularly where it requires a different department, as you have now identified further dependencies and more stop-starts. Challenge these. Rework and defects usually lie beneath the radar, so make sure you map them – and measure them too.

8. The Waste of Talent or Skills

Some years ago I visited a small company who made parts for the boating industry. During my visit, the MD introduced me to Lucy, a 23 year old sales person. He proudly let me know that she singlehandedly generated 50% of the total sales of her team of 4. When I spoke to Lucy, I could see why. She had tremendous people skills, and I could well imagine her building strong relationships with clients.

So I asked her, if she had a magic button that she could press to get rid of anything that got in the way of her doing her job, what would it be?

Without hesitation, she replied, 'Friday afternoon. I *hate* Friday afternoons! Our receptionist goes home at 12, I sit on the third floor and every time someone rings the bell I have to go downstairs, see who it is, then if they have an appointment, I take them upstairs to their contact. I get no work done on a Friday afternoon.'

The MD looked like he had been smacked in the face by a wet fish. Here was his prize sales person, and she was losing two working days a month by answering the door! This is a classic example of the Waste of Talent. I'm quite sure that in her interview, no one asked her how good she was at climbing stairs.

Before the end of the day, he called me in to say that the problem had been sorted, he had arranged with a contractor to come in and fit a video camera and remote door-opening system the following day. 'Lucy will never have to get up to answer that door again,' he assured me.

'John, that's great,' I answered him. 'You've just done a Lean improvement. However, there is an important question you need to ask yourself.

Why did it take the MD to make it happen?'

This made him swallow hard. But it is a critical question for any chief to answer: why are your managers allowing obvious issues to continue unresolved, even when they consume ridiculous amounts of time for their most productive team members?

Why are you wasting the talent of the people you employ, by letting them do ridiculously wasteful tasks?

The truth is that these managers are Busy People.

But remember, any fool can be busy. It's being effective that counts.

Lucy's manager saw the problem but prioritised his work over resolving her problem. This is simply wrong. As her manager, he should have been setting her up to succeed as much as possible.

I once witnessed a disgraceful scene in a meeting, where a manager said she didn't have time to sort out a technical issue that was requiring a separate team to manually scan 600 pages of barcodes every few days to update the system. This process should have been automated almost 3 years earlier, when the system was rolled out. You should never be too busy to eliminate mindless tasks from a team, even if they are not *your* team.

The Waste of Talent is a dangerous waste, because your best people will quickly feel undervalued and may move on.

THE ACID TEST FOR WASTE

Discussing the types of waste with a team is a powerful way for teams to understand the need to change. If anyone is ever unsure of whether a step is wasteful, ask them: 'If everything were working perfectly, would this step be required?'

If the answer is No, then it must be waste.

Notes

Good Lean Practices

Incremental improvements

During my sandwich degree, I did a 6 month work placement at British Aerospace (now BAe Systems). I worked on the final assembly of the BAe 146 aircraft. I remember that everyone on site loved that aeroplane, and took a real pride in what they did. My job as an undergraduate was to help create a visual management board that tracked the status of every mechanical, electrical, paint and upholstery job needed to finish a plane during Final Assembly. The production managers used this board during each of their shift changes, to agree the plan for the day, understand progress and identify key issues. Anything that couldn't be quickly resolved at the board was taken off-line and reported on at the next meeting.

What I took from that time was that manufacturing was really about good problem solving. Also, how meetings were far more effective with good visual management. And finally, how easily problem solving stalled when faced with big challenges. My boss was a young, clever guy called Steve, and he told me how everyone got hung up about the tail assembly. 'They all say the problem with Final Assembly is the tail plane. The thing is, the issues around the tail plane will take years to resolve and cost a fortune.

There are hundreds of things we could just be getting on with right now, that cost nothing and could be done in an hour.'

Steve went to do a Fellowship in Manufacturing Management at Cranfield University (years later I would do the same) and I took over co-ordinating the production meetings. I found I really enjoyed learning about the day to day problems that arose on the line, and liked the challenge of working with people across the organisation to fix them.

But that lesson from Steve has always stayed with me. Lots of small, incremental improvements are way better than one big improvement that takes forever, especially when you are trying to turn around culture. People can see and be motivated by small improvements, but that one big change … by the time you've implemented it, everyone's lost interest and the world has changed, so that it may no longer be that important anyway.

Continuous improvement helps you get better at implementation. It also means that culturally, an organisation begins to get confident at handling change, because it becomes the normal way of doing things. This means there is less resistance to change generally, and the improvements you make are far more likely to be sustained.

Kaizen is the well-known Japanese term for continuous improvement, and was a key component of the Toyota Production System. Continuous improvement or Kaizen is simply about being a little better today than you were yesterday. If you want to visualise the power of this, picture a grain of rice on a corner chessboard square. Now imagine that each square has double

> The other advantage to an incremental approach is that you can quickly understand how to improve your change process because you get feedback sooner. How well did you build relationships, did the communication work, did you use the right measures, did the training work well, were stakeholders kept informed … and so on. It is vital that a team continually gets *and acts on* feedback so that it continuously improves.
>
> As we'll see later, this is the Plan Do Check Act concept and is exactly how Scrum teams work.

the amount of rice on it than the one before. So the next square has 2 grains, the one after 4, and so on. If each grain represents a tiny insignificant improvement, you will be staggered when you calculate the number of grains of rice that will be on the 64th square.

The point is that the cumulative effect of tiny so-called insignificant improvements can lead to massive transformational change.

A Learning Organisation

One of the things I consistently find again and again with organisations (particularly large organisations) is that their culture is poorly set up to learn from the past in order to improve the present and the future.

For example, Joe's team was seen to have messed up the launch of a new system, but instead of inviting Joe and his team and other key players to have an honest and open discussion around how to improve the process next time, the department manager makes some disparaging remarks about Joe's team, or allows these to be made by other team leaders when Joe isn't around. This creates huge levels of distrust. Since Joe wasn't given the opportunity to explain that the specification had been incomplete, or there had been many last minute changes that his team had not been empowered to refuse, he and his team feel unfairly treated. They become demoralised and a 'them and us' atmosphere prevails. As a result of this blame culture, everyone becomes fearful of new system rollouts, the process gets extra checks and reviews 'just in case', meetings are battle grounds, it becomes easier to live with substandard, overly-complex applications rather than fix them, people point fingers instead of collaborating to solve problems, and innovative thinking grinds to a halt.

People have surprisingly long memories when it comes to being treated unfairly. It has an enduring effect on how a team feels about itself, and how it responds to its internal customers and suppliers. In my experience, the only way to move forward with this team is to replace the department manager with one who is prepared to listen to the issues, respect people, and support and facilitate solutions rather than focus on discovering so-called culprits.

A Learning Organisation thinks of a problem as an opportunity to improve, rather than as an obstacle to overcome, or a person to beat up. If you see problems as opportunities, you will naturally become good at problem solving. And an organisation with strong problem solving skills will much more easily develop a culture of continuous improvement, which as we've seen, is a key principle of Lean.

FAIL FAST

One thing that the Agile community brings into play is the principle of **'fail fast'**. Scrum teams receive rapid feedback from the customer because they demonstrate real working software on a regular basis. You 'fail fast' when you demo something the customer doesn't want. This is a good thing! You found out early on that it wasn't right and stopped wasting your time. You applied this knowledge to the next piece of work so it deepened your understanding of the requirements.

Teams should continually challenge themselves to improve. Not just their processes, but how they work as a team, their systems, how they communicate, how effective their meetings are … in other words, a good team has the courage to analyse itself and take the required action to change. Any unnecessary waste is identified and removed. For example, a meeting that adds no value is shelved. A visual board that causes confusion is improved. Not later. Now. One great team I worked with had a simple but effective mantra: 'Now is good.'

With Lean improvements, if you try something like a new tool or system or process change, and it doesn't work, drop it. Don't waste time on stuff that doesn't work out. You will always gain knowledge from failure. There is no such thing as negative experience at work. Understand what went wrong and use the knowledge it gave you.

A Learning Organisation is one whose people are resilient enough and bold enough to move on from so-called failures and become even better as a result of them.

Honest conversations

It's important that people are willing to have difficult conversations in the quest for improvement. If the feeling is that someone messed up, then another team member should be able to respectfully raise the issue openly with that person. If relevant, review how the process could be improved to help prevent the same thing happening again. Talking collaboratively about removing waste and preventing process errors stops it feeling like a personal attack. The point is that difficult conversations, well handled, build trust. Problems left unresolved and unvoiced will ferment, and ultimately affect the team's performance.

Being respectfully honest is one of the biggest compliments you can pay someone, because you are trusting them to make good use of the information. I once received some very valuable feedback from a great colleague on how I had poorly handled a disruptive person in my meeting. The feedback was painful but the knowledge it gave me was something I could use for the rest of my life. It made me realise that honesty from someone you trust is a gift.

I learned that rather than getting upset at the poor behaviour, I should have calmly described the impact it was having: 'You are continually

As a junior change agent many years ago, I had carefully managed the change for a new process, but the daily production meetings demonstrated that the handover to the business had not worked well. If there was an issue with the new process, the production managers would raise it and look expectantly at me to resolve it. This was two months after launch! It dawned on me that they had never taken ownership, and this was my fault and also my responsibility to fix. I took a deep breath in one of our meetings to explain that a) if I was the only person on site responsible for change then we would all fail and b) they owned the process. I had set it up, agreed it with them, trialled it, trained everyone, launched it and resolved any issues. The fact that their teams were not using it properly was not something I was going to help them with. As production managers, this was their responsibility. It was a very honest speech, and from then on, the new way of working was fully supported by them.

interrupting people, and raising your voice, which is starting to make the discussion shut down. Why is this?' Note that it is important to use facts when describing the behaviour. You can't say, 'You're rude', or 'You're disruptive' because these are your own perceptions. And by using facts, you are getting their logical brain to respond, which tends to get better results.

It's important to then listen to and understand the response: 'I feel I'm not being heard as I've raised concerns that seem to have been ignored.' Now you can understand the behaviour, you need to find a reasonable solution: 'This meeting is an ideas meeting so we are not here to discuss constraints and 'what ifs', just ideas. Otherwise we stop the creative flow! Let's list out any risks next time.' And the grievance has been aired and resolved.

It's all about being respectful without compromising on results.

But if poor behaviour continues, then take that person to one side and say, 'I am happy for you to come to my meeting, but it *is* my meeting and I need you to be prepared to collaborate. If you are not able to do this, you should consider whether you best serve this company by spending your time elsewhere.'

Honesty has a big impact on the success of Agile transformations. On a regular basis the team are expected to identify ways that they can directly improve how they work together, and these changes are applied with immediate effect. There is no such thing as a post-project wash-up with Agile. You focus on getting better as you go along. Why wait until the end? This review is impossible to do well unless there is an atmosphere of honesty and trust. When the team members feel constrained from airing their true thoughts, the opportunities to continuously improve will always diminish.

An organisation needs leaders that actively encourage respectful and honest dialogue early on when things (or relationships) aren't working. If it fails in this, it will not become Lean, because it is not a Learning Organisation.

Plan Do Check Act (PDCA)

One way to help a company become a Learning Organisation is the Plan Do Check Act cycle. PDCA (also called Plan Do Study Act, or PDSA) was made popular by the quality guru Edward Deming in the 1950's and is as relevant today as it was then.

> In Scrum teams, this PDCA meeting is formally held at the end of each sprint (a sprint is usually 2 weeks of concentrated effort around achieving a small goal) and is termed a Retrospective. The Retrospective asks how the team could continuously improve how it works. The mantra is 'Inspect and Adapt'. It is seen as a hugely important aspect of Scrum, and is *not* something the team fits in around its core work. It *is* the core work.

The PDCA cycle can be used to fundamentally change your culture. Just identify one thing you want to improve, grab a small team, draw up a flipchart and create a simple visual plan of action. Then do. Then check you are achieving what you said you would. If not, act. Repeat daily.

This PDCA means that a team becomes very good at challenging itself to do better. If this means that a team member tells Angela that the reason nothing was achieved in week 3 (Plan, Do, Check) was because she didn't delegate before she went on holiday, fair enough. Angela might need to ask herself why she didn't trust her team enough to delegate. As their manager, she should be invested in improving their skills. Maybe she needs to book herself some leadership training (Act). Her team realises that she values their input, and is prepared to take it on board and improve. The team goes from strength to strength.

Does your company talk rather than do?

Another common culture you may need to challenge is the culture of talking rather than doing. Far too many organisations are greatly invested in *talking*. That's fine up to a point, where talking is ensuring you are involving the right stakeholders, and actively collaborating. It is *not* fine when nothing ever changes as a result. Nothing is more depressing than sitting in the 10th meeting where managers talk about the issues and *nothing changes*. Stop having those meetings. Right now. They are a huge source of waste in an organisation, and they frustrate everyone.

I once met with a company that spent 12 months explaining Lean to everyone, and doing process maps to show waste, before any actual improvements were carried out. This is nonsense. By the time Lean

> My first challenge when I organise a meeting is how to cut the time in half. Ideally, I then cut it in half again. This forces me to think how I am going to communicate key information ahead of time, and how I am going to visually display our thinking and decisions during our time together. I also start every meeting with a reminder of what the objective is for that meeting. Simple principles but they really work.

came their way, everyone had forgotten what it meant, and they didn't believe anything would change. Plus, the processes – and the world–had moved on. Talking is always easier than doing.

I have previously mentioned that I was once stores manager at an aircraft galley manufacturer. The company made fleets of galleys and stowage units for Boeing and Airbus commercial aircraft. The company was a bit of a tin shed with a leaky roof, but it had the most abundance of common sense I have ever seen in a work place. People were excellent at everyday problem solving, and this was led from the top. There were 250 employees but the MD knew every person's name. Every director made good decisions on the hoof. It had some of the best managers I have ever worked with. As stores manager, in a year I only attended a 20 minute production meeting every morning, one improvement meeting every other Friday with the ops director, and I got pulled into maybe 2 other meetings that entire year. The rest of the time I was free to just do my job. That company had a great ability to get things done, helped by not tying everyone up in meetings.

The company I went to next manufactured aircraft seats. What a shock! I spent a minimum of 3 *hours daily* in meetings with other senior managers and the MD, going over each contract part by part to see where the shortages were. We were basically the most highly paid expeditors on the planet. The waste was beyond belief, as was the blame culture. I spent so much time in meetings that I had no time to spend with my own team. I lasted just 3 months before I gave up and left.

We would have been far better off setting up visual boards for the actual expeditors to update so that we could see at a glance how the seats were progressing. It would have eliminated the vast majority of those meetings. I truly believe that had we not wasted so much time talking about the issues, and then repeating it all the next day, we would have had the time to think of this! But it was in my pre-Lean days.

In 2000 I was Business Improvement manager at another aircraft interiors company where we had a very engaging, positive MD, and everyone was very hard working and collaborative. *But* we really struggled to turn ideas into reality. Every issue went on a backburner, because there didn't seem time in the day to complete the daily work, let alone make improvements! Of course, as you start to address the items that cause waste, you begin to free up time, but it's hard to make a start. We were classic 'busy people'. Again, lots of meetings about problems, but not a lot seemed to change!

A change agent called Nicky B joined us, and made a very simple difference to how we worked. He listened to some of the problems a department was complaining about and drew up a visual plan on a flipchart in the form of a table with some simple headings – Action No (1,2,3,4 etc); What (the action required); Who (the owner of the action); When (due date) and a final column for Comments. He created a small task force from that department and others to fix the problem and this team held 5 minute stand-up meetings around the board, every day. Essentially, it was a PDCA process. Completing this plan was the only document that the team created other than a few measures – no Gantt chart, no minutes, nothing else. Just the flipchart. It meant that the team owned the plan, could clearly see accountability and progress and were motivated. When did you last see a team motivated by a Gantt chart?

In just 10 days the team had identified the key issues, implemented all the quick wins, checked the measures were demonstrating success, and were already working on some of the longer-term issues that would address root causes. The

> You don't just have to use this visual tool for improvement projects. I use it as a daily planning board with operational teams. Give me 10 minutes a day standing up around a board, reviewing a simple plan as part of PDCA, over 1 hour a week in a meeting room, any time. Agile teams will *always* have a short daily stand-up for this reason. It really works.

position of that flipchart was key to this success. It was in the centre of the room, visible to all. The fact that it was a stand-up meeting, taking just a few minutes per day, was also paramount to its success.

Soon, these flipcharts became the way we worked there. A strict rule was that we were not to use whiteboards, only flipcharts. This was so that any due dates that had slipped could not be conveniently wiped off. We had slipped into the genteel habit of giving dates but not sticking to them. Now that that habit became visible to our peers, we dropped it. That meant that things *actually happened*. In a short time, we changed from a company that talked to a company that did.

This was a massive, transformational change for us. It forced everyone to raise their game. It also introduced us to the power of visual management.

An interesting side effect to the boards was that directors became more interested in operational issues. Quite often a director would 'happen' to be walking past during a stand-up, and he or she would stay and listen. This wasn't to poke questions at people, or check up on them, but it did help ensure that people lived up to their promises. I personally felt that a number of our directors had been too shy to ask questions previously, perhaps for fear that their lack of operational understanding would be exposed, and the boards gave them a way in. They came and looked, and saw what people were up to, and gained a better understanding of what was going on. It also helped convince them when asking for funding to solve the bigger issues!

Senior managers should ask themselves – If someone had a great idea today for an improvement, how long would it take to get it in place? If one's heart sinks at the answer, your senior team need to realise they are preventing rather than enabling change.

Easy as pie?

We tend to simplify our everyday lives very nicely. It's only when we get to work that stuff seems to get complicated. I once came in from work, cooked an apple pie from scratch, had a shower, got changed, took the pie and some cream and went to a friend's for dinner. All of this was accomplished within 60 minutes of walking in the door. Perfect flow, you could say. Of course, I didn't have to rely on anyone else to get it done.

Wouldn't it be great if you could do the same thing at work? Just get on with the one thing you want to focus on, and just do that until it is done? Not have any dependency on anyone else to play their part, at the right time, and at the right level?

The work place is an imperfect place. We do have to collaborate with others, as we can't have all the skills ourselves to do all the work all of the time. And of course, everyone else has their own priorities. Lean organisations understand this, and spend a lot of time on ensuring that teams work effectively together by making the work and the priorities clear and visible. Teams share responsibility for the apple pie. And everyone on that team knows exactly what their role is in making the pie, and what the pie should look and taste like.

Now let's compare this with a non-Lean organisation. That 1 hour becomes 3 days, because there was an apple shortage, and someone had ordered the wrong flour because the recipe was unclear. The person in charge of peeling apples had another job to finish first. The purchasing manager was stuck in a meeting and unable to authorise expediting charges. Someone had to check with 6 people as to which pie they wanted. Plus the pie inspection was held up by a priority job for a special customer who later turned out not to want pie after all.

There is a lot of noise in non-Lean organisations.

One of the best ways to start to improve the flow of work is to eliminate all unnecessary dependencies. The more dependencies you have, the more discussions you are going to need to get stuff done. The more priorities you will come up against. The more delays you will experience. The more stop-starts.

As a manager, helping your team remove dependencies – including where they are overly dependent upon *you* – is a good way to start with Lean. Look at the number of pairs of hands that the process goes through and challenge whether these are all truly adding value. And every time someone has to ask you to make a day to day decision, ask yourself why they can't decide this for themselves. What can you change about the process, or introduce with respect to visual management? How can you best empower your team to make daily decisions without you?

One company I helped was forever complaining about its suppliers being always late on delivery. I discovered that the date on our purchase orders was not the date that the supplier received the order, it was merely the date that the PO was created by the buyer. Sometimes there was a delay of up to a week before the PO was emailed to the supplier! As many parts had short leadtimes, this certainly didn't help the suppliers deliver on time.

By mapping the process, I discovered that the final step was the quality manager signing off the PO. I asked why.

'A couple of years ago one of our buyers was put under pressure by production to buy a part quickly, and he bought it from a non-approved supplier. By having all POs come to me, I can be sure that we are only using aerospace-standard providers.'

Just then, a buyer rang and said that she needed her PO approved as it needed to go out urgently. He dug through the email folder, added his electronic signature to the PO and sent it out without even checking it. So what was the point of this extra step?

Instead of ensuring the system only allowed a buyer to raise a PO from a pre-approved supplier, using a dropdown list, a new step was added, involving a whole new department and adding up to 5 days delay! And if the quality manager was away, it didn't even go to a team email address. (Inept solutions such as these are far more common than you might think).

Lean training helped explain the waste that this step was generating. A number of steps were wiped out with the removal of that dependency and the supplier gained up to 5 extra days to make parts. Late deliveries were greatly reduced at zero cost.

SECAR

There is an acronym called SECAR, which I find is a very simple and effective way to challenge a process.

S means Simplify.

E means Eliminate. Take out any steps or resources that add no value.

C means Combine. If you can put two or more steps together so one person can do them, you remove dependencies. I describe this as 'removing pairs of hands'. The more pairs of hands, the more stop-starts, the greater the need for communication, and the harder it is to maintain flow.

A means Automate. Get the system to do the hard work. The example in the box above used the system to error proof the process. But always ensure you Lean the process first. Otherwise automating it will simply lock in existing waste.

R means Relocate. Moving a step to a different point in the process can make a big difference. This is especially helpful when trying to error proof. When you take out cash from an ATM, you take your card out first, *then* it gives you your money. Imagine how many cards would be left in ATM machines if cash were given first!

I used SECAR recently with a urology team in a hospital, to further improve their one-stop haematuria clinic. Currently, the patient arrived, had a nursing assessment followed by a scope and the consultant decided at that point whether a CT scan or ultrasound was required. Once they'd had this, the patient had to wait for an appointment that afternoon with the consultant to review the scan or ultrasound results. The scopes were done in the morning and the follow-up appointments in the afternoon. This allowed time for the scan reports to be done.

So a patient would arrive at 9 am and leave around 3 pm. So although it was termed a one-stop, it was still a very long day for the patient.

Using SECAR, the team changed the process. The consultant would decide which type of scan to use *before* the patient arrived. This decision was based upon the health of the patient, and the consultant already reviewed this information ahead of time, so they could make the scanning decision then too. It meant that the patient could be assessed and then scanned on arrival. Making the decision ahead of time meant that proper slots could be created for the patients in each scanning department. Thus when the consultant scoped the patient, the scan results were already available and he or she could discuss the findings with the patient straight after the scope.

It meant we:

1. *Relocated* the scanning decision and also the scanning itself to the front of the process
2. *Combined* the scoping step with the patient consultation, but
3. *Eliminated* the afternoon appointment so that most patients could go home at the end of the morning. For elderly, unwell patients (and their carers) this meant a great deal. It also freed up the consultant's time in the afternoon to run a separate clinic and reduce patient waiting times.

Quality Assurance versus Quality Control

We have already looked at the Waste of Rework and Defects. A common mistake is to think that Quality Control is the answer to reducing defects in the system. Put inspection points in, and you'll find them. But statistically speaking, if your process allows defects, you will never find all of them. You cannot inspect quality into a product or service. Instead, the goal should be to prevent defects happening in the first place.

This is the key difference between Quality Control and Quality Assurance. For every £10 I have, I would spend £1 on checking for defects (Quality Control), and £9 on preventing them at source (Quality Assurance).

> Before we had Chip and PIN, it was incumbent upon a shop assistant to spot that a customer's signature was fake (QC). There was a great degree of process variation, depending on how closely the assistant compared the card signature with that of the customer's, and how disposed the assistant was towards challenging that customer. And so fraud flourished. Once a customer had to key in a PIN, that variation was eliminated – quite simply, the assistant was no longer part of the verification process.
>
> The point is that Chip and PIN is a QA improvement. Rather than having to increase anti-fraud activity, the payment is prevented at source.

Using a ticket inspector on the train is Quality Control. Using ticket barriers so you have to swipe a valid ticket before you can get onto the platform is Quality Assurance. Creating standard procedures, visual management, effective training and communication are examples of QA. Carrying out audits to check people are working correctly is QC.

Preventing defects happening in the first place is hugely effective. It's impossible to be Lean without thinking Right First Time. It's impossible to get to Right First Time without focusing on prevention rather than cure. The impact of good QA practices will always be to reduce the Waste of Rework.

Note that you cannot deliver quickly on a consistent basis if there is a big risk of introducing defects into the process. QA plays a big part in creating consistency, which helps to give a solid platform on which to build further improvements.

Poka Yoke

The Japanese use the term Poka Yoke for error proofing. It's not meant for something that helps reduce the error rate – it is when you actually eliminate the cause of the error. I grew up in an era where every electrical appliance was provided without a plug. When you bought an iron, you had to wire in the plug yourself at home. A lot of effort was put into making this wiring easier, but fundamentally, nothing would stop you from wiring the plug incorrectly. Diagrams were provided, the wires were colour coded and school children taught how to wire plugs in science lessons, but mistakes still happened.

Then appliances were provided with moulded plugs. The errors were eliminated.

Another example of Poka Yoke in the home is your toaster. Most toasters will not allow you to push the lever down if the toaster is unplugged. This prevents you believing your toast was heating up when it wasn't. If only kettles were as sensible. Most of them just give a light to show they are plugged in, which you can easily miss.

There are lots of safety features on London Underground trains to reduce error rates, but an example of Poka Yoke at Jubilee station is that it's impossible to fall in front of a train because there are doors between the platform edge and the train, which only open when the train has stopped.

Look at your processes and identify where the Quality Control points are. Ask yourself where Quality Assurance plays a part. Now ask whether there is any way you

> I would like to see a standard fuel tank design used by all car manufacturers and pump manufacturers that makes it impossible for a diesel hose to be used for an unleaded vehicle's fuel tank, and vice versa. The hoses and pumps are colour coded, fuel caps are labelled, but 150,000 users still put the wrong type of fuel in their cars every year in the UK.

can introduce Poka Yoke so that errors are eliminated rather than reduced. The earlier this happens in the process, the more the Waste of Rework and Defects will be reduced.

Measure for success

I once worked on an improvement project to reduce the lead-time for repairing and testing coffee makers, ovens and rice cookers for airlines. We reduced the lead-time of the old process from 30 days to 4 hours, and we did it by eliminating manual handling, mapping the process, challenging waste and redesigning the equipment and layout of the cell.

The process originally had the customer send a zero-value purchase order along with the part. The operator inspected the item, generated a Bill of Materials for the parts needed for the repair, and a labour estimate. The part then went onto a rack while the sales department costed the work, and contacted the customer to confirm they were happy to accept the price. The customer would amend the PO to the proper amount, production control created a work order, ordered in the parts and sent them to the operator, who now completed the job. This was often 3 weeks after it had been put to one side. A clear example of the Waste of Waiting and Delays.

By analysing the process, I could see that in 5 years a tiny percentage of repairs had been turned down, and these were all for high cost items. Also, 80% of the repairs were very similar in price. Yet 10 days out of the 4 week lead-time was waiting for sales to contact the customer and for the customer to confirm the go-ahead and amend the PO.

We made a radical process change. The operator would complete the repair, rather than have this stop-start each time. We let our customers know that we would charge a standard price for a standard repair so their POs arrived at that amount at the start. The operators inspected the part, created their own work orders and managed their own parts, so we eliminated production control from the process. For standard repairs, there was no stopping. For very complex repairs only, they stopped and consulted with the customer via sales. This reduced the dependency on sales.

The cell was created over a 4 month period and customer satisfaction levels soared. The operators loved it as the zero manual handling eliminated all of their back problems. 80% of the parts flowed through the process without stopping. Everyone was happy. The project was a complete success.

Two years later, our ops director's replacement asked me to prove the reduction in lead-time. I had deleted my calculations and the IT system had been completely overhauled. That taught me a valuable lesson – always document your measures properly and include them as part of the project file!

Please don't measure for measure's sake. I once visited a company who had a 'measurement wall'. It was about 30 foot long and held a wealth of measures relating to their supplier performance over the last 2 years. I walked to the start and the end of the wall. The performance levels had increased by about 2% in that time. Measures should drive tangible results or what is the point of doing them?

In the NHS, over a 15 year period, the number of staff appraisals increased by 71%, but the number of employees who believed their appraisals were effective in helping them do their jobs increased by just 3%. With measures, always be wary of ticking the box and missing the point.

Focus on a few good measures which show the story of what is happening. Here, the key measure was customer lead-time from point of order receipt to point of delivery. However, I would always recommend measuring Quality, Cost *and* Delivery. So we measured Right First Time based on the number of units that failed final test after the repair stage, as well as any errors made, and customer complaints. We tracked costs against sales to ensure our new pricing system was giving a good profit margin. If you focus on delivery alone, for example, you will deliver faster but you might simply have increased your overtime levels and reduced quality to do so!

Use pull rather than push with your measures. In other words, start with what you will need to know at the end, and at what level you will need to know it. Think of your car dashboard. You don't need to know the temperature of your car engine – you just need to know if it gets too hot. Let the level of information required pull the measures you need, rather than setting up a whole series of measures and hoping some turn out to be useful later on.

A key advantage of having good measures is that it becomes increasingly easy to win the hearts and minds battle against change. You can *prove* there is a problem with current state and increasingly, you will be able to *prove* that your previous changes made a difference. It's a lot harder to argue against change when the evidence for it is compelling.

It also takes a lot of the emotion out of a change, when you bring measurement data into the argument. Remember that with change, you are proposing to alter a system or a process that someone else worked really hard to create. If that person is still at the organisation, it is unavoidable that they will be emotionally invested in the current state, and it is entirely reasonable that they resist and even resent the change. Sometimes it can feel like you are telling a parent that their baby is ugly! Gently showing the data, as well as genuinely explaining the features you are going to keep, will go a long way to getting them on your side.

I was lucky enough to have the late Martin Westray as my mentor at Cranfield. He told me of a great story involving measures.

His client was an MD who was fed up with his admin teams not working hard enough (as he saw it). He insisted on setting up a measure to check their output – every day at 4pm, every administrator had to count the number of items left in their in-tray and report it in a spreadsheet. 'This will do the trick, Martin,' he said gleefully. Martin tried unsuccessfully to stop him. He pointed out that it was a fairly meaningless measure because you could have one item of work that would take you 3 hrs to do, or 10 items taking 5 minutes each! But the MD insisted that just putting in a measurement would drive an improvement in itself (agreed, but make it a fair and meaningful measure!).

The next time Martin visited, the MD was ecstatic about the success of his trial – it had caused an 80% productivity improvement. People were getting on top of their in-trays and the number of items left undone each day had gone down dramatically. 'I told you it would work!'

Martin had a nose round the company before he left, and stuck his head in the door of a very busy room that he hadn't noticed previously.

'What happens in here?' he asked.

'Post room,' was the reply. 'We've expanded to cope with our internal mail. It's gone through the roof!'

Guess what? Just before 4pm every afternoon, people were emptying the contents of their in-trays into an envelope and sending it back to themselves via the internal mail. Then first thing every morning, they would just open their envelope and pop the contents back into their in-tray before starting work. I promise this is a true story.

Show me a poor measure, and I'll show you a behaviour you didn't want.

Lean Consumption

Lean consumption looks at waste from the point where the customer starts the process, to where they finish. Its philosophy is that the customer's journey always begins before your company's process starts. Remember that example from earlier, where we hired a car from the airport and mapped the process with the waste? A Lean consumption process map would start right at the beginning, and include your customer getting a quote for the car hire, and how easy it was to complete the online form, and how straightforward it was to reset their password and ask any questions. This is the biggest difference between Lean consumption and the Waste of Over Processing. Otherwise they are very similar.

How Lean is your customer able to be when consuming your goods or service? Do you force them to jump through unnecessary hoops? Do you waste their time?

Imagine that your boiler has broken down, and you need to contact your boiler repair scheme's call centre. The call centre takes ages answering your call and then insists that you need to give them the make and model of the boiler – despite the fact that their company installed the boiler! Only the make is on the boiler, but not the model number, so you have to end the call and trawl through your paperwork to find the boiler details on the purchase order or service records before you can even register a breakdown. You finally get through again and the boiler repair person turns up the next afternoon, as promised. Unfortunately, the part that needs replacing needs to be picked up from the warehouse, so they have to reschedule to come back and fit it three days later, when they next have a slot. Not great for a customer without hot water or central heating.

Let's look at this with Lean consumption eyes.

The process failed because the customer had to jump through hoops before they could even report a problem to the call centre. The process also failed because the call centre handler didn't ask the correct questions to accurately pinpoint the likely cause of the breakdown. Had they been given more technical training, or a flow chart for questioning, the fault could have been narrowed down to a few likely options and the corresponding parts taken with the repair agent on the initial visit. That's Lean, as the chances are it would only have taken one visit and one conversation to repair the boiler.

So making these improvements would reduce the Wastes of Waiting and Delays and People and Parts Movement, and re-training the call centre operators to add more value to their role would reduce the Waste of Talent. Never lose sight of the fact that the only value-added step in this entire process is 'fix hot water and heating'.

Chapter Six

5 S

5 S is a fundamental building block of Lean. It is a Japanese methodology for organising your environment and it absolutely applies to your everyday life as well. In fact, we tend to 5 S our homes without even thinking about it. 5 S means 'a place for everything and everything in its place'.

Here are the 5 S's – Sort, Set, Shine, Standardise and Sustain. (I personally believe we are missing a 6th one – Simplify).

Sort

'Sort' means getting rid of anything that adds no value. (The tidying up expert Marie Kondo is an expert in this).

In a factory, you would do a 'red tag' exercise at this step. Everyone puts tags on any item that is no longer used, and it definitely works best if everyone is involved, not just the shopfloor. I once did this with a company who were about to spend £100k on buying the factory next door, as they didn't have enough space to operate. The red tags showed that we could walk 150 feet along the production line before seeing any machines actually in use. There were also parts that had been made out of the wrong material sitting around in case they ever got an order for them. Guess what? This company didn't need to spend money renting out more space. They just needed to get rid of the stuff that added no value.

It's important to physically move tagged items into a separate holding area. It's a psychological thing. Move out the clutter so you can see the potential for the space left behind. Some of the home improvement shows use this concept with homeowners before the change. Move out possessions, spray paint everything white, and now the space is so de-personalised that it is easy to see how it can be better used.

I advise giving people a hard deadline of 2 weeks to make a case for keeping a red tagged item. It has to be a valid case. Not just 'in case someone wants it one day'. On that principle, you'd need a separate factory just to house spare items. Paper is one of the best things to challenge, because a paper-based system always involves the Waste of Waiting and Delays while you look for information.

Then stick to the deadline. Make a record of what you no longer need. Otherwise 5 S will be the culprit for the next 15 years every time something goes missing. Then get creative and do something inspirational with the items. Donate computers and old desks to a local charity. Give stationery to schools. Publicise this. Your employees like to know that in a bad old world, they have been part of something good.

5 S is all around us.

Do a 'Sort' on your wardrobe. Sell anything you haven't worn in the last year. 'Sort' your filing. 'Sort' your garden shed. A so-called friend who likes to put you down? Rarely makes you feel good? Why are you making time for this person when you barely have time to see the people who make you happy? 'Sort' them from your life. Today!

Set

Now you have got rid of everything that adds no value, set out the remaining items such that you minimise wasted movement and delays. Use something all the time? Put it next to you. Use something rarely? Why is it taking up precious space on your desk? Move it to a cupboard. You have

At the aerospace interiors company, our change agent Nicky B implemented 5 S. His first step was genius. He started with the MD, 5 S'd his office with him and got rid of the waste bin. Why are you throwing stuff in the bin? It has to be waste. You are accepting failure! He then challenged him to question every piece of paper that landed on his desk. Does it add value or not? And if it does, did it need to be printed out? Paper is a precious commodity for this planet. It also needs to be handled, sorted, filed, looked at and often creates waste for others. These simple actions set the tone for 5 S company-wide. There was only one waste bin per floor after that. It made us think more about what we were discarding when we had to get up and walk to the bin.

It was the first time at the company that continuous improvement had been applied to the offices as well as the shopfloor. Everyone in the organisation was trained in the concept of 5 S, and understood that a red tagging exercise was required. The office staff did clear out a lot of unwanted stuff, but they still held onto lots of things 'just in case'.

So Nicky made them a promise. He set up part of the stores as a big holding area, put a gate on it and put the key to the padlock on the gate in his pocket. He told everyone that this was the 'archive' area. If anyone was worried about actually throwing something away, in case they needed it later, they could 'archive' it, and if at any time it was needed, he would personally fetch it for them without delay.

People agreed to this plan, and he filled this huge space with files, drawings, catalogues, filing cabinets full of previous employees' documents and so on. With the freed-up space, we re-laid out the office in a logical flow, and seated the right people together to ensure the most effective communication. It created a real improvement buzz.

I asked him a year later how many times he had had to fetch something from the 'archive' and he grinned broadly. 'Not even once!' Apparently even the effort of ringing him made people think twice as to whether or not they really needed their file (despite previous assurances that these were critical items). Shortly afterwards we threw everything away or donated it, dismantled the area and there was not a murmur from a single soul. Most people had forgotten the stuff was even up there.

This taught me that 5 S is not just about tidying up and organising yourself and your work. It gets you mentally ready for change. When the space was freed up, people could see its full potential. They could see beyond the As-Is. They would never have done this if we had just presented them with a floor plan and asked for ideas. Getting rid of physical clutter actually frees you from mental clutter. That's why spring cleaning a house is cathartic.

Nicky once said to me, **'5 S is the preparation of the mindset for the philosophy of continuous improvement.'**

I completely agree.

Imagine you are selling your home. A key reason why a well -maintained, well-priced property does not sell is because it contains too much personal stuff. Those cardboard boxes piled up in the spare bedroom? Those knick-knacks on every surface? That conservatory used as a dumping ground for bikes? They prevent a buyer from really seeing the *value* of these rooms.

So first SORT them, and then SET out your house so that each room contributes the maximum amount of value-add for your buyer. Put a shed in the garden and transform the conservatory into a dining room. Otherwise it's the most expensive bike storage ever. Set out every room for its maximum potential.

My friend was struggling to sell her two bedroomed flat. The second bedroom contained a cot and a lot of boxes. I advised her to empty it out and put in a double futon. The flat sold in two days, purely because people could now visualise a double room. They could see the value of the space because she had applied SORT and SET.

sorted any system files that you no longer use. Now identify the handful of files you use almost all the time and make them accessible within a keyclick.

Since 5 S means 'a place for everything and everything in its place' you need to store everything in the correct place so that you find it quickly when you need to. 5 S is a great starting point for Lean, which is why I always begin with 5 S when I help factories implement Lean. A manufacturing consultant once commented to me that 5 S is 'the fluffy stuff'. This guy once ran a machine shop! 5 S is a fundamental starting point for machine shops everywhere. Out of date tooling binned. Most commonly used items to hand. Machines laid out to minimise effort and movement. This stuff is not difficult but being well organised is fundamental to being Lean.

5 S has been a standard technique in operating theatres since they were invented. Who ever saw a surgeon hunt for a scalpel?

That de-cluttered wardrobe? Set out your remaining items so you can clearly see them, eg by colour or by type. Set out your kitchen to minimise movement. I have a drawer that contains only 10 items. But they are the 10 items I use all the time. Nothing else is allowed in that drawer! And when my baby was born, my whole nappy-changing area was 5 S with everything set out in order of use. My husband laughed at me until he had to get up at 2 am and do a nappy change. Then it made perfect sense!

5 S doesn't just apply to the physical world. A well-designed website will have only the information you need, just where you need it (Sort and Set). This will minimise the waste of clicking through pages looking for something. Similarly, organising your electronic files will save you time. 5 S is strongly connected to the Wastes of People Movement, Transport and Waiting and Delays.

Shine

Everything counts when it comes to first impressions. You don't just judge a restaurant on its food, you base it upon the entire experience. Imagine you visit their toilets and they are dirty. I have left restaurants before ordering for this exact reason. And yes, it is possible that I have missed out on some great cuisine. But my thinking is – if you can't keep your toilets clean, I don't want to eat your food.

> **EVERYTHING COUNTS**
>
> How would you feel if you were in a doctor's waiting room and all the plants were dying? Think about the assumption you would make about the level of care you were about to receive. Subconsciously you would think, if you can't even water your plants, how are you going to take care of your patients?

Our assumptions are often not logical. One airline made me feel exceptionally nervous throughout the flight. When I examined the reason, I realised that its staff were scruffily dressed. Completely illogically, I felt that an airline who didn't care about the personal standards of its staff would be careless about the safety of its plane.

Standardise

Once you have achieved the right level, standardise throughout. There's no point creating a fantastic kitchen if the rest of the house is full of clutter. There is no point in vastly improving part of the process, if the rest of the process is still rubbish. What difference will your customer experience? It is generally better to make small improvements end to end, than a huge improvement for just one step. When I worked with London Underground, we needed to ensure that all lines delivered a service in the snow and ice. Having one great line didn't count. No customer was going to say, 'Well my tube broke down at Victoria, and there were delays on the Northern so it took ages to get to work … but wasn't the Central Line fantastic today?'

World class companies get really good at creating standards and being very clear about their expectations. When I was working with McLaren, we discussed their clean desk, perfect factory policy and the planning manager explained, 'When someone comes to interview, we tell them: this is how it is. If you don't like it, don't come to work here.'

And when VIPs visit them, there's no tidying up beforehand. They maintain that place at a showroom standard all the time. When I was at the paint factory, it amazed me that a visit from other European plant managers necessitated a major 5 day clean-up operation. How wasteful. Production managers organising cleaning crews instead of focusing on delivering product. We should have maintained a high level at all times as our standard.

When you standardise, you set out your stall for 'That's how we do things around here.' Setting standards means that you spot quickly when there is a problem, anomaly, or deterioration, and you can address it fast.

That's why I don't like the term '5 S exercise'. If you are doing an exercise in 5 S, you are not a 5 S organisation. Anyone can look great for a day. It's meaningless.

Sustain

Ask a group of people which of the 5 S's are the hardest to achieve, and they are likely to answer 'Sustain'. This is true. But here's the thing. The more you standardise the new ways of working, the easier it becomes to sustain the change.

5 S is exceptionally powerful. That's why it is such a strong corner-stone of Lean. They are both about changing how you think, so you can transform your world, not just improve it.

Here's a true story from my time at Cranfield of how 5 S totally transformed a business.

A small company in the north of the UK manufactured and installed its own boilers in people's homes. Their problem was that they had a large range of boilers, all designed by themselves. And lots and lots of stock of a wide range of individual components. But they never had the right stock at the right time. It was a case of having 95% of the parts, but without the missing components, they couldn't even start to build.

Because of this, boilers took up to 6 weeks to build once they received an order, and because there were so many designs, not every engineer could install every boiler, so there were waiting times to install, too. They were losing orders. As one customer memorably put it, 'By the time you give me my boiler, winter will be over!'

The company engaged the help of a Cranfield consultant, whose first step was to challenge them to reduce the range of boilers on offer. He wanted the company to offer just three types – let's call them cheap, medium and expensive. Obviously, the expensive version had the most

> I believe the most important 5 S is Standardise. I often tell teams that being consistently poor is a far better starting point for Lean than being inconsistently great. You have a standard performance platform on which to build your improvements and you already know your weak points. Being great every now and then, or just within parts of the process, can create unwarranted complacency.

functionality and efficiency. In effect, they carried out a 'Sort' on the range of boilers offered.

The other big change was standardising the boiler design, so they all had the same base design and componentry. This meant that the cheap and medium boilers had *the same components* as the expensive option. For the expensive boilers, all the components would be wired in, medium boilers would have only some of the components wired in, and for the cheap ones, there would be very little further wiring, as hardly any of the additional components would be connected. The base model was designed to locate the components such that their wiring could be done at the end of the manufacturing process. This is a 5 S 'Set'. This important step meant that 95% of production for *all* boilers was the same and therefore production was able to be standardised.

'You're crazy!' they told him. 'Why are we adding redundant components to our boilers? We are basically going to give away components for free. You've just added cost for no reason to our cheap and medium products!'

But he convinced them that by creating a standard product, you remove complexity from the process. You are now dealing with a very simple manufacturing process. You can *afford* to give away these components as your entire product is massively cheaper to make. Fewer types of components means higher volumes, which equals lower procurement and expediting costs. It also means fewer shortages and better customer service levels. Such is the power of standardisation.

(In fact, car manufacture is very similar as it uses a technique called mass customisation. When you buy a lower range model, you may notice that not all the features work on the dashboard. For example, some have lights that are simply not used. This is because the final wiring takes account of the model you have paid for and only wires those components in your specification. Having a standard dashboard, with built-in redundancies, is far cheaper overall than keeping a separate part for each variation. You design a standard, but customise by order at the end).

The company built a small level of stock of the basic boiler model, operating a simple pull system to make more when the stock ran below an agreed limit. (These are called Kanbans, as explained later). All they had to do when they received an order was pull a base model from stock, check the order to see what kind of boiler had been ordered, do the final wiring and testing, and arrange for it to be installed. As the processes were so standard, every engineer was trained to install each of the 3 types of boiler.

The leadtime dropped from 6 weeks to 4 days.

Sort the redundant designs and components. *Set* out the new design so that you have a new *standard,* ensuring that all of the wiring can be done at the end. *Shine* your installation engineers and their vans so that they give the best impression.

Was the change *sustained?*

Well, actually they improved upon it.

Within 6 months, the installation engineers were trained to carry out the final wiring and testing *at the customer's home,* and their van equipped with the materials and equipment needed. This meant that a boiler could potentially be installed within 24 hours of the order receipt. The engineer just had to check his or her schedule to see what type of boiler was required, take a standard boiler out of his or her van and complete the wiring and testing required.

The leadtime dropped further from 4 days to 1 day.

Never underestimate the power of 5 S.

Notes

Structured Problem Solving

I believe one of the most defining characteristics of a Lean company is the ability of its people to solve problems well. Lean organisations actively develop this skill amongst their employees. Non-Lean organisations rarely do, in my experience. There's a lot of firing from the hip, making assumptions rather than getting the facts, and solving today's problem, all of which are examples of poor – as well as lazy – leadership.

An example of poor problem solving: a few years ago I was working for a public service organisation, and our change director had been asked to help with the restructuring of a department. I was asked to join her project team as an advisor.

At our first meeting, I asked a very simple question. It's usually the first one I ask. 'What is the problem we are trying to solve?'

The director's answer: 'The head of the department says his current team structure isn't working.' She pulled up an organisational model. 'Let's put in this. It's a standard blueprint for that kind of department.'

I asked, 'How do we know for sure that the problem is with the team structure?'

She looked affronted. 'The department head says so. And he *is* the customer!'

I tried again. 'But what information do we have to back this up? And how bad is the problem? What sort of issues is he facing?' I was genuinely baffled.

Because in reality, the conversation was a joke. If you can't define and quantify the problem, how can you attempt to solve it? How can you be sure you have made an improvement, when you haven't even measured or understood the baseline? Who's to say the current structure doesn't work because, say, the department head is ineffective and needs leadership training, or his managers do? We should have been spending time with the team, really understanding their issues, before jumping in with an out of the box solution.

Our director could not answer my questions but blindly insisted on moving forward with implementing her model. Finally after a couple more meetings I was forced to say, 'I don't buy into how we are approaching the problem. In fact, we don't even know for sure what the problem *is*, and unless there's a compelling reason for me being here, I'm going to leave.' I got up and left the room. And the project.

I have never regretted walking away when I fundamentally disagree with the approach. I *have* regretted staying on projects that I didn't buy into, or that undermined my values. Don't do it.

To be an effective change leader, it is essential that you are able to problem solve effectively. The method I use is the Structured Problem Solving Wheel, which I learnt at Cranfield. It beats all others hands-down. The Six Sigma DMAIC is useful for data driven problems, but if you want a tool that you can use with a team to solve problems daily in *and* out of work, this is the one.

Structured Problem Solving Wheel

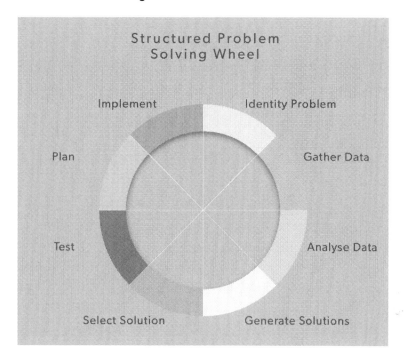

Structured Problem Solving Wheel

Implement

Identity Problem

Plan

Gather Data

Test

Analyse Data

Select Solution

Generate Solutions

1. Identify Problem

Write the problem in a sentence. I often start with the words 'How do we ...' as I find this makes for simpler wording and a shorter debate. Stay high level, and don't include solutions in your statement. Don't spend hours wrangling over the wording, because you may well go back and reword it when your team have understood the problem better anyway.

You would be surprised at the number of teams I have facilitated, who are happy to continue to have meetings without having a clear agreement of the problem. It's crucial that everyone on the team understands this. Defining the problem is so important as it focuses the team and lets everyone check their understanding of what they are trying to achieve.

2. Gather Data

Now we know what problem we are trying to solve, we start to gather data around the current situation. A problem is a gap between where we are and where we want to be. What facts do we have about that gap?

Let's say a problem is that a hospital's theatres are always running late. We could identify the problem as 'how do we improve the schedule adherence of our operating theatres by 15% in the next 60 days?' We obviously need to have data to show current performance levels and create an agreed baseline against which the change will be measured.

Not all of the data is quantifiable. If team morale amongst theatre staff seems a problem, you might also design a short survey that would help you understand the issues and provide another baseline. For example, 'From 1-10, how likely are you to recommend working here to a friend, and why?' The why isn't quantified but is just as important to understand as the score. You can then repeat this survey 3 months down the line and apply PDCA.

Measures show you how big the gap is, and can help to pinpoint the issues causing it. However, process mapping is probably the most useful way of gathering data, as it forces the team to stand back and understand the detail of how the work is currently done, and where the waste is. Value stream mapping is useful to see where the delays are, but my preferred method is standard swim lane process mapping to show handovers, rework loops and dependencies. I would always go and

> My son's English teacher told his class a story about 5 blind men. Each blind man touched a part of an elephant, and was asked to describe it. The one touching the tail described it as a piece of rope, the one touching the ears thought they were a piece of cloth, and so on. The point is, no one knew they were touching an elephant because they were only focused on their own part.
>
> An end to end process map is an excellent data gathering tool, but one of its key strengths is where people work in silos and have little understanding of how the process works up and downstream of them. It shows everyone the whole elephant, so to speak.

see the process for myself if I were mapping it with a team, to observe it end to end and talk to everyone involved. Not just the nurses, junior doctors, surgeons and anaesthetists, but the health care assistants, administrators and patients too. Everyone who touches the process needs to be listened to.

Never make assumptions. Never trust important information given to you that isn't backed up by facts, or by at least by two independent sources. Information is *not* the same as wisdom. Gathering data means just that.

3. Analyse Data

Take the data you have gathered in the previous step, and look at what it tells you. Gather more data around the wastes that you have uncovered. This is what I call the 'So what?' phase of problem solving. There will be a lot of waste, but can we measure the impact to understand what to tackle first?

The goal is to identify some of the underlying causes, so that you can focus your efforts on solving them in the subsequent steps. The 'Five Whys' are useful here. Just keep asking Why and see if you get to the bottom of things. (I once had a client who asked me to explain the 'Five Wives'! By the gentle smiles on the faces of his team, I saw how much they treasured working with him).

Why do we run late in theatres?
Because our patients aren't ready on time.

Why?
Because our nurses aren't here when we need them.

Why?
Because they are short staffed with getting the patients undressed and prepped.

Why?
Because the health care assistants are running around sorting stock shortages and organising additional equipment.

Why?

Because there are last minute changes to the theatre schedule
so things had changed when they walked in the door at 7am.

So there is a key issue worth investigating–the theatre schedule isn't truly locked down ahead of time so everyone is reactive rather than proactive at the start of the day. You need to understand how often this happens, uncover the underlying causes, and measure the impact this all has on the theatre schedule adherence. I would recommend using an Ishikawa or Fishbone tool for this. The Effect would be 'late schedule changes' and you would get a big team to identify and categorise the Causes of this. It can help uncover root causes that you then address. When all roads lead to Rome, therein lies a root cause.

4. Generate Solutions

We often forget to be creative at work. We park in the same spot every day, sit in the same chair in a meeting, and take the same approach to problem solving that our company's culture has always had. Remember that Einstein defined insanity as doing the same thing over and over again, but expecting different results. When I have a change team, I try to add at least one person who has nothing to do with the process, so they can give a different perspective.

When you start this step, don't block creativity by stating your own opinion. The minute you do that, you stifle the discussion. The really clever thing about change is not to be the clever person. Try to give everyone space to talk first before you say anything at all.

Let's say that after doing a lot of root cause analysis in step 3, you have discovered the single biggest reason for late schedule changes, and can prove that fixing this issue would have the biggest impact on theatres running on time. You now need to identify a number of ways to solve this issue.

Do make sure the team generates a number of options, rather than diving to the obvious. The single biggest mistake people make is that they have a 3 step problem solving method: Identify problem; Select solution; Implement. And they often don't even do the first one right. This is especially common with new senior managers wanting to quickly make a mark, as follows:

- Identify problem (yes, I've seen this before)
- Select solution (here's what my last company did)
- Implement – (just do it, I tell you!)

They actually force the problem to fit their solution. It never works. It skims the surface of the issues because they didn't tackle the root causes. It can cause even more pain. Don't let this be you.

Encourage teams to use 'What if?' and 'What else?' I really like these phrases, as they open up the discussion. Get the message across that no suggestion is worthless, and all have value. If you find someone is being negative, here are some techniques I like to use. For example, Alex has just given you three reasons why a great idea can't be done:

1. 'So Alex, what you are saying is that *if* we fix the issue with the system, *and* we explain it to everyone, *and* we don't put it in at the same time as we do the other change so we avoid confusion, then it's a good idea and will work.'
2. 'It's not carved in stone. Why don't we try it for 4 weeks and review? Plan, Do, Check, Act.
3. 'Can you just explain when *would* be a good time to do it?'
4. 'If our competitors came up with it, and managed to increase market share with it, *then* would it be a good idea?'
5. 'Okay, thank you for that, so what's your solution?'

5. Select Solution

Simple. Choose the best solution out of all of those generated. And if you select the solution and some team members feel that there's too big a compromise somewhere, you didn't do step 4 well enough. Compromise is the cancer of success, so go back and generate more options.

6, 7 & 8. Test, Plan and Implement

These steps are bunched together because you know what they mean.

Congratulations! You have now systematically identified and removed the biggest barrier to theatre schedule adherence. Measure again, review the effect of your improvement (PDCA) and tackle the next biggest barrier if you still have some way to go to achieve your improvement goal.

The Dangers of Poor Problem Solving

A word of warning. When I was Continuous Improvement manager at the paint factory, the European head of production decided she would bring in some external consultants to evaluate our production lines and identify how we could increase productivity.

There must have been at least 4 of these guys and I swear that they were with us for 6 *weeks* and *not once* did I see any of them step onto the shopfloor. Not once. They sat in a room and crunched numbers on their computers all day long.

Then there came the big presentation from the consultants to the senior site team, on their findings. Now, we had three shifts operating on the shopfloor: morning (A shift), afternoon (B shift) and night (C shift). These consultants took an hour to walk us through all their calculations and showed about 30 slides with very colourful graphs on them, and they all seemed to indicate that A shift was the problem shift. Graph after graph showed that these operators had the lowest productivity of any of the others.

Recommendations? More training required for A shift. More support staff needed. More frequent performance appraisals. Ramped-up quality audits. And so on.

Kitty, our European head of production's boss was there, a woman whom I held in high regard. She said nothing for a few minutes, and then turned to the plant production manager, a very experienced man called Alan. It struck me that, like myself, this was the first time Alan was seeing the output of these consultants.

'Alan, what do you think?' asked Kitty.

Alan took a moment, and then shrugged his shoulders. 'No engineers on nights,' was all he said.

A pause, and then we all got it. No engineers on nights meant that any problems on C shift had to wait until the morning. When A shift came in to start work, they would be faced with engineers trying to recreate and fix the problems of the night before, and this would undoubtedly disrupt their lines, resulting in lost productivity.

Instead of understanding and focusing on solving the maintenance staffing issues, the consultants had cast A shift as culprits.

The point is, data is meaningless unless you understand it. You need to get away from your desk and stack of spreadsheets and *go to Gemba* – a Japanese expression meaning 'where the work is done'. (Although never use that expression out loud. Another consultant once told me I needed to go to Gemba and it made me want to shove my sandwich in their face).

Those consultants? They were on site just long enough to collect their jackets, when that presentation was over. I can still see their faces after Alan said that one line.

Another word of warning.

Don't always assume you need a big problem solving exercise to get the job done.

Back to the paint factory. One problem was the robot stacker. This stood at the end of each paint line, stacking full paint cans onto the pallets as they came off the line. The robot interleaved each layer of paint cans with a sheet of paper, and then put a sheet of card on top of the top layer of cans before shrink wrapping the whole lot. However, one of the robots always broke down. Whenever I checked, there would be two or three demoralised operators hand-stacking tins of paint on a pallet, while an engineer scratched his or her head and tried to reboot the robot to make it work. You've probably picked up a few 2.5 litre paint cans in your time. No big deal, right? But have you picked up, turned 90 degrees and stacked 250 of them onto a pallet? Only one or two layers are the right height for your back. The rest are too low or too high. You also have to reach to the back of the pallet to stack. And all the time you are doing this, you are fully aware that this is a boring, meaningless, ridiculous job because *there is a very expensive robot that should be doing it!*

It seemed to me that there was little sense of failure around what was happening. I felt that if our management team had had to stack cans for just one shift, the problem would have been sorted a lot faster!

So I started asking questions.

It turned out that the robot almost always broke down while it was laying the final sheet of card. The good news was that at least the pallet was fully loaded. The bad news was that it took an average of four hours to get the robot running again, and that meant that subsequent pallets had to be hand-stacked with the remaining cans, or the line would be blocked.

The company had spent tens of thousands of pounds in lost productivity, maintenance, spare parts and labour to that machine. No one knew why that last layer of card was so problematic. So I asked what seemed to me to be the obvious question – why do we need the last layer of card? Why don't we just leave it off?

The answer was – 'We need it because otherwise the top layer of paint cans would get really dirty in the warehouse, and our customers would complain.'

I had already booked a trip to the warehouse, because I wanted to see the next step in the paint production process. Once there, I watched as one of our lorries made a delivery, and 10 minutes after the pallets were unloaded into their new locations, a young storeman came around with a picking list. He walked up to our newly delivered pallet, tore off the shrink wrap, then pulled off the top layer of card and threw it in the recycling bin! He then selected two cans of paint and added them to his trolley.

> **KEEP IT SIMPLE**
>
> A core principle of Agile is that 'simplicity is the art of maximising the work not done'. This sounds strange until you realise that maximising the work not done is exactly what you are achieving in a situation like the one above, when you *don't* spend 3 months on a project that could be done in a day, because you asked the right question in the first place.
>
> Of course, this Agile principle directly aligns with the Waste of Over Production.

So there was no way we really needed that top piece of card! It turned out the storemen often tore off the top layer within hours of a pallet arriving, and we had never received a single customer complaint about dirty paint cans–although we *had* received plenty of complaints (and fines) around paint cans not being available when required in stores. Probably because they were being hand-stacked.

So we changed the problem to, 'How quickly can we re-programme the robots to remove that last op?' and it was done in a day. 90% of the problems with the robots stopped. Who cares why the last card made it fail? Just get rid of the card!

A final note – we were delivering hundreds of thousands of pallets a year. That final layer of card was costing us £20,000 *per year* in materials. So not only did we save our operators and engineers valuable time and increase their productivity and morale, we also took £20k off the bottom line of our operating costs by reducing the inventory of paper. Plus fewer trees were cut down for such a meaningless cause.

Notes

Controlling Work in Progress using Lean

Creating flow is a huge part of being Lean. One of the most powerful changes you can make in an organisation is to stand back, and try to get the work to flow faster and right first time.

As we have already seen, Lean is about identifying the value that is being created and treating everything else as waste. By eliminating as much waste as you can, you start to flow the work from value-added step to value-added step. But you should also look at reducing batch sizes to reduce waiting times, and limit inventory by introducing pull systems.

Why do we break down batches?

Think of lifts as opposed to escalators. With lifts, people stop and wait and then get moved as a batch. Escalators move or flow individuals continuously as a batch size of 1 (known as single piece flow).

It has been mentioned that reducing batch sizes is a key way to improve the flow of work through a process. In manufacturing, batch sizes are reduced wherever possible because wherever you have batching, you *must* have queueing. This is because the first item waits for the last to be finished before it can move to the next stage. Batches are easy to spot, because you can see where the physical work builds up.

Batching is much harder to spot – and its damage much more difficult to convey – in a service industry. Why is batching a problem here?

Well, imagine your doctor writes you a referral letter for an operation, but your doctor's surgery only sends out referral letters on a Friday, instead of daily. So they collect them at reception and send them in a batch to the hospital once a week. This means that if you had a GP appointment on Monday, a consultant would wait at least 4 days to receive that letter. Now imagine that the consultants review referrals on a Tuesday and Thursday, and they only run a clinic every other Tuesday, and you can see how queue times very quickly build up as a result of batching.

(By the way, this doesn't happen. GP referrals are sent electronically to hospitals).

One lady I worked with told me emphatically that the organisation she worked for did not batch.

I asked her what her job role was.

'Learning and Development manager.'

I asked her to describe the induction process.

Of course, it is often impractical to eliminate batching entirely. A batch size of 1 will not always be realistic. You don't write a single Christmas card, address it, stamp it, walk to the post box to post it and then repeat with the next card. But a batch size of 50 almost certainly involves part-finishing and stop-start. The time from start to finish of all 50 cards can be weeks!

However, if you use a batch size of 5, then you will find it easy to complete and post 5 a day. In 10 days you will have finished, and you will have been spreading the joy from day 1!

In Agile, this is a simple example of the concept of continuous delivery of value.

'We wait until we have about 15 new starters and then we run a 1 day induction programme.'

I asked her what was the longest period a new starter had waited for their induction.

'Yes, that *is* something that people complain about. One person waited for 6 months before we had enough people to do the course!'

Guess what? I said. That's batching. I suggested she challenged the content of the induction to ensure it included only those elements that added value, and ran it with 5 people instead of 15. This would greatly shorten the queue time for an induction. (I don't like inductions where you do all the training online, or you are on your own. It's a good opportunity to meet other new people and get a sense of the culture).

Push vs Pull

As mentioned previously, if there are high levels of work in progress (wip), you are almost certainly looking at a push operation. Push means you are simply pushing work into the system, regardless of when it will be worked on by anyone else. Most companies that have not implemented Lean use push systems, and suffer accordingly from the Waste of Over Production. People work hard, but the work just piles up part-finished and they find it difficult to deliver on time.

So a way to control wip levels is to look for opportunities to change to pull and only move work into and through the system when resources are ready. Don't do it until you need to, then do it fast.

Let's say you have a washing machine, tumble dryer and laundry basket at home. A *push* system would be where you ran the washing machine irrespective of whether the tumble dryer was free to take the load. Wet washing piles up in front of the tumble dryer as you continue to use the washing machine. Your washing machine is working really hard, but fundamentally you won't be getting clean, dry clothes any quicker into your laundry basket at the end of the process!

A *pull* system is how most of us operate in the home, with one load in the dryer and one in the washing machine. As the dryer is emptied, it *pulls* the batch of wet clothes from the washing machine. The washing machine then *pulls* the clothes from the dirty linen basket and starts a new wash cycle. Yes, dirty clothes might pile up in the linen basket, but you don't continue to wash them if

> A simple example of a push system in the work place is with data. Typically, dozens and dozens of reports are created in organisations and circulated (pushed) to long lists of recipients. How many people actually use that information? A *pull* system would be a self-service platform for users to customise the fields and run a report only if and when they wanted to.

there is no capacity to dry. Everything works together, limiting wip in the system.

Bottlenecks

As previously mentioned, a bottleneck is a resource that does not have enough capacity for the work it needs to do. What is key is that a bottleneck will always determine the rate of output.

Think of the washing machine, tumble dryer and laundry basket in the section above. If the tumble dryer takes twice as long to dry the clothes than the washing machine takes to wash them, you won't get any more clean clothes in your laundry basket by going out and buying a faster washing machine.

It's the dryer you need to focus on. It's the bottleneck.

To increase output, you should put all your energy into reducing the bottleneck. So challenge whether everything needs to go through the dryer – put underwear on a radiator, and put towels and sheets on a clothes airer. It's far better for the environment anyway. Now you have challenged the bottleneck, you will have increased its output and therefore the output of the entire process.

I highly recommend reading **The Goal** by Eliyahu Goldratt, which goes into detail of how to manage bottlenecks using his Theory of Constraints.

A common mistake when working on bottlenecks is just to look at one part of the process, without looking at the bigger picture. Years ago, I worked alongside a team of consultants at a bank, improving their customer complaints process. Our team was tasked with reducing bottlenecks in the Claims Review phase, which was the first step in the process. However, it was clear to me that the Claims Redress step further downstream was far more broken, as the work just seemed to grind to a halt at this stage.

Sure enough, we made the work move faster at the front end, and it just got stuck in Claims Redress. We should have focused on fixing the biggest bottleneck first. Our efforts in speeding up Claims Review made zero difference to the customer's experience. At the time I was new to the team and didn't want to rock the boat by making this suggestion. I later kicked myself for it. This experience taught me to always speak up when I believe a team is focusing on the wrong thing.

Kanbans

Kanbans take the concept of pull a step further. They are a Japanese manufacturing technique and are visual signals which trigger a pull action. They are very often used as part of a Lean transformation, because they help improve flow and minimise wip by controlling it.

A Kanban minimises the Waste of Inventory, by ensuring that you only produce or buy what you need, when you need it. This is exactly the principle of Just In Time systems (JIT). In the example of supermarkets earlier, with regard to suppliers getting a signal from the checkout to replenish stocks when they fall below a certain level, this signal is a Kanban. The Kanban controls the wip, because a supplier cannot simply overload the shelves.

To illustrate Kanbans, I often get teams to create a two bin Kanban for their stationery. The stationery cupboard contains a row of small boxes, each neatly labelled with the item description and maximum quantity allowed (eg 30 red pens). Each box has a replica box behind holding an identical amount of the same item (this is the second bin). Once the front box is empty, this acts as a signal to 'pull' the box behind and switch it with the empty box. The empty box gets refilled during the next week or so. The rule is to only pull items from the front box and a daily check is done for items needing replenishment. Hurray! No more running out of stationery, which means no more hoarding by employees who are scared of running out of staples.

Most people keep one tube of toothpaste in the bathroom, and a spare tube in a cupboard. Once the main toothpaste tube is empty, it acts as a visual signal that you need to 'pull' your spare tube from the cupboard to replace it and then buy (pull) more toothpaste to replenish your backup.

In other words, the bathroom cabinet and cupboard act as a two bin Kanban. The level of inventory in the system is reduced–you don't need more than two tubes of toothpaste, because if you follow the process, you will never run out.

This kind of Kanban can reduce a company's stationery costs by thousands of pounds a year because inventory is minimised.

My son's electronic payment system at his school is another example of Kanban. I can set a minimum limit, and if his account balance falls below this limit, the system is triggered to automatically 'pull' a small sum of money from my bank account to top it up, so he never runs short of lunch money.

McDonalds' replenishment system is based on Kanbans. You probably don't go there if you have a 2 hour lunch break, or want somewhere comfortable–unless you need free Wi-Fi. But McDonalds are very clear that part of the value that they deliver is in fast, consistent-tasting food. McDonalds operators use flexible Kanbans to build small levels of stock during peak periods. As the items are sold, they are replenished via Kanbans. This careful building of stock means they can quickly react to a spike in customer demand, but are still able to keep low levels of wip to reduce food waste and ensure it tastes the same each time.

The important point is that in a production line, Kanbans exercise control by preventing an operator from continuing to work if the downstream process is not ready to receive it. The operator will physically stop working rather than build more wip, if they have reached the limit defined by the Kanban. This exact same concept is used in Agile Kanban boards, as we will see later.

Notes

Chapter Nine

What is Agile?

Agile is a philosophy and a way of working and thinking that was developed by the software development community and is based partly upon the principles of Lean.

There are 5 principles for *what* Lean is, but *how* you achieve a Lean transformation is not defined by these principles. Using the right Lean tools together with the right cultural changes will help you get there, as explained in the first 8 Chapters of this book.

In the same way, Agile has 12 core principles for *what* Agile is, but *how* you achieve Agile working is not defined by these principles. Furthermore, unlike Lean, there is no hard and fast definition for Agile. Instead it is quite loosely defined by its 12 core principles, which are collectively known as the Agile Manifesto, and are as follows:

1. Customer satisfaction through early and continuous delivery of useful software
2. Welcome changing requirements
3. Frequently delivered software
4. Close, daily co-operation between business people and developers

5. Projects are built around motivated individuals, who should be trusted
6. Face to face conversation is the best form of communication (co-location)
7. Working software is the primary measure of progress
8. Sustainable development which is able to maintain a constant pace
9. Continuous attention to technical excellence and good design
10. Simplicity is essential and is the art of maximising the work not done
11. Self-organising teams
12. Excellence through reflection

A number of these evoke the philosophy of Lean. A focus on customer satisfaction. Face to face conversation rather than lengthy documents and emails. Excellence through reflection is similar to continuously seeking perfection, the 5th principle of Lean. Simplicity ... is the art of maximising the work not done. This means removing unnecessary work, so it is closely related to addressing the Waste of Over Production. Note that there is nothing in the Manifesto that dictates that wip levels should be reduced, or batch sizes lowered. It also says nothing about pull rather than push. Yet companies who successfully practice Agile working will almost certainly have achieved this.

Where Agile differs most to Lean is in its emphasis on early and continuous delivery to the customer, and being responsive to changing circumstances. As I said earlier, Agile is about creating customer value faster and responding to change.

Agile software development teams use different frameworks to *how* they approach Agile working. Two of these frameworks are Kanban and Scrum. The other frameworks are very specific to software development, so I will ignore them, but the concepts used by Kanban and Scrum can be applied to *any* organisation to optimise improvements or full-scale transformations when combined with Lean.

The next 2 chapters explain how these frameworks are used in Agile software development. We need to understand this before we can see how they can be used in non-IT environments.

Notes

Agile via Kanban

Where a software product or service is delivered over short timescales, or the team has to tightly control work in progress (wip) or where the plan frequently changes, an Agile software development team will probably use a Kanban framework via a Kanban board to manage and deliver the work.

Kanban boards are an Agile tool based on Kanban pull systems in Lean. These boards are used by a team to visualise and control the work flowing through the standard steps of a process. Each step has a column on the board–low tech versions are simply flipcharts with post-its moving along the labelled columns as the steps are completed.

The Kanban team will have a 10 minute daily stand-up around the board to agree the plan for the day and how to handle any impediments (obstacles) to the work. The business customer often attends along with any other interested stakeholders, and answers any questions the team may have. This connects the person wanting the work with the people doing the work, and ensures any misunderstandings are quickly resolved. Note however that it's the team themselves who run the meeting.

A Kanban board's fundamental principle is that if you continue to accept work into your system, it will slow down the work you already have. Therefore, only a pre-defined level of wip is allowed in the system at any one time. Work is done in order of priority, as defined by the business customer, and the team moves each item across the board until it is done. The customer can change the priority, but they can't insist on more work being accepted into the system than the team can handle.

Kanban teams are empowered to switch off the tap at the front end and focus on completing the work they have already accepted into the system.

Make no mistake, Agile Kanban is a massive change for managers who are used to just piling the work onto their teams, then wondering why it takes so long to be delivered.

How does a Kanban board work?

There are strict rules around starting new work without existing work being completed.

These rules are implemented by the use of *wip limits* for each step in the process. Each process step has its own column on the board. The wip limit shows the maximum amount of wip that is allowed in that column at any time, and is shown at the top of each column heading. These wip limits prevent a build-up of part-finished work anywhere in the system, **as no more work can be pulled into a column if its wip limit has been reached.**

Usually there is a column 0 to the left of the board called Waiting to Start, which can have unlimited wip, but the items on it are sorted in order of priority by the business customer.

Let's say there are 5 steps to a process, represented by columns 1-5, and each column has a wip limit of 2 items of work. This means the team has agreed that the maximum amount of wip allowed in the whole system at any one time is 10 items. The team will always focus its effort from right to left, since Column 5 contains the work that is closest to completion so it should be prioritised. If at any point a wip limit is reached, no more work can be pulled into that column until an item of work has moved on. The team will self-organise and may decide to move resource to tackle the bottleneck and improve flow.

Higher wip limits generally mean the team expect to have a certain amount of stop-starts with their work, so they allow a small number of other tasks to be worked on at the same time. The lower the wip limits can be, the faster the flow of work across the board. Create too high a wip limit and you have a board that allows too much wip in the system, and you will slow down. I would advise a middle-lane approach – this is Agile, and you can change the wip limits following an Inspect and Adapt cycle until they work best for you.

A photograph of a very simple Kanban board that I helped a team to create very recently appears on page 92. I include it so you can see how this tool can built in just a few minutes. Once the team has used it a few times and the wip limits seem about right, I would recommend re-building it in Trello, or keeping it as a post-it version if the team is co-located.

Kanban boards are a powerful tool in getting teams to work together end to end to flow the work. They also force items on hold to be addressed rather than put to one side – there will be a rule for the number of On Hold items allowed at any one time.

A Kanban team's mantra is **Stop starting and start finishing.** Finish the work that is already in wip before you begin anything else.

How many tasks are you working on right now? If you have just one thing to focus on, you will be 100% effective. Given two tasks, you will be about 80% effective. By the time you have 5 key tasks you will be 50% effective at most. That's right: half of your time will be spent trying to remember where you left off, reworking errors made from part-finished work, relearning information, and trying to remember what you did previously.

None of this adds value. Context switching is hugely wasteful. A Kanban board seeks to eliminate this waste by minimising the work in progress within the team, helping them focus on a small number of items at a time.

Final Data Gathering WL = 4	Training Env WL = 6	Final change WL = 2	Final sign-off for Live WL = 4	Move to Live WL = 2
Urology rebooking	Endoscopy rebooking	Urology Tci	HRAC	
Dermatology Tci	Respiratory Referral	Pulmonary Embolus		
MSK Follow up	Biologics			
	Breast clinic			
	MSK forms x6			

If situations change, the boards are responsive because the Waiting to Start column can be re-prioritised by the customer by just moving the items into a different order. If work is already in wip, it can be moved by the customer to the top of its column so it will be worked next. If it is urgent, such as a sudden system failure, the team can start it immediately. However, there will be a limit and an agreed criteria to the number of urgent items allowed at any time. Without rules such as these, every item suddenly becomes urgent and the board is unworkable.

What I find powerful with Kanban boards is that the work can move so fast that it is completed before anyone can change their mind and re-prioritise it! Where work takes ages to deliver is when excessive decision-making around priorities comes into play.

Kanban boards complement Lean working as work (value) flows and teams self-organise with the minimum of communication and decision making. They need the minimum of time spent in meetings. Roles and responsibilities are clear – the business owner is the What and the team is the How. Prioritising the work does not fall onto the team, it is down to the business owner, who also sees very clearly and transparently what the team is doing so is not endlessly bombarding them for status updates. Note that no project manager role is required!

With Agile teams using a Kanban approach, there is generally less focus than Lean teams on removing waste from the process. For example, challenging whether the 5 steps could be reduced to 4 is generally not addressed by an Agile Kanban team. They are often more focused on flowing the work through to delivery than questioning the process itself.

Why not do both? Eliminate any process waste, as per Lean. Empower the team to self-organise and stop starting and start finishing, as per Agile. Using both Lean and Agile will optimise delivery of the work.

Remember, it is only a Kanban board if wip limits are used, as this is the only thing that is providing the pull. Otherwise, you just have a tracking board and you are not reducing the Waste of Inventory. You are simply watching it.

EXAMPLE OF AN AGILE KANBAN BOARD

Let's use the airport car rental company from earlier as an example.

Imagine there are 3 employees tasked with getting the cars ready for customers flying into the airport with pre-booked cars. The team works to today's flight schedule, in order of arrival. Fred cleans the cars' interiors, Jo washes them, and Sue does the paperwork.

Now, there's no point Fred being 5 cars ahead of Jo. Or Sue being far ahead of them both on admin. Their customers can't drive a car away until all 3 steps are complete. So they set up a Kanban board with four columns – Waiting to Start, Clean, Wash and Admin.

Let's say they agree a wip limit of 2 cars each for Clean and Wash, and 4 cars for Admin, which is faster, to balance the flow. Each car has a post-it on the board with the car reg plate on it and flight arrival time. At the beginning of the morning shift, all of the post-its are in Waiting to Start in flight arrival order. Fred pulls the first post-it into the Clean column and starts cleaning his first car. He then moves it into the Wash column and pulls in another post-it into the Clean column. Jo begins to wash the first car.

Half an hour later, Fred finishes cleaning his current car and sees that Jo still has 2 post-its in Wash. He pulls a second post-it into his column and begins to clean the second car. He finishes it but Jo still has 2 post-its in her column, as she had a problem with the water supply. Fred's blocked from starting any more cars because both he and Jo have reached their wip limit. Fred uses the board to decide whom he should help. If Sue on Admin has also hit her wip limit, she will be his priority. Not much point in him helping Jo only for her to be blocked because Sue is behind! Otherwise he will help Jo catch up.

Sue has reached her wip limit of 4 items in Admin, so Fred helps her and she is able to complete a car. She then pulls Jo's first car into the Admin column, which frees Jo up to pull Fred's first car into Wash, and Fred is able to continue by pulling a new post-it into his Clean column, and so on.

The team is self-organising because every member can see the bottlenecks and move to help a colleague address them without any management intervention. All the information they need for effective decision-making is there.

This concept of self-organising is critical to success with Agile. The team must be empowered and trained to flexibly move around as the work requires. The team must also be empowered to re-schedule the order of work or adjust wip limits if they are not well balanced for any reason. They use 'Inspect and Adapt' to continually improve how they work as a team.

Agile via Scrum

In software development, the Scrum framework is used as an approach to Agile where the product is complex and will be delivered over a number of weeks or months, and the team is able to plan their work for the next 1-4 weeks without responding to constantly changing goal posts. The Scrum team will consist of a Scrum master, whose role is to serve the team by facilitating effective working, and software developers/testers. There is also the product owner, who is the business customer of the end product. The product owner prioritises the overall work and makes decisions regarding the requirements, based on demos at the end of each sprint. The product owner is also responsible for communicating with stakeholders so as to canvas opinion and keep key players in the loop, but he or she is the ultimate decision maker, and *the only customer voice into the Scrum team.*

A key principle of Scrum is that the work is broken down into 'chunks' and the list of chunks is called the product backlog. A Scrum team will use sprints to manage the product backlog.

Sprints

Typically a sprint is a 2 week time frame where the Scrum team work to achieve an agreed goal. Note that some teams use sprints of just 1 week, and others use 4 week sprints. Usually, a 4 week sprint indicates a team is confident that the sprint goal is very stable, and that the team has a good understanding of the requirements. A 1 week sprint would mean more frequent feedback from the product owner, so less risk of rework, and the team can absorb a greater level of disruption from changing requirements. If there is too much disruption, however, the team would probably be advised to use Kanban instead, as per the previous chapter. (And please note, there is nothing stopping a Kanban team also using sprints to plan their work – I frequently do this to get the best of both worlds. Simply change the Waiting to Start column to Approved for Sprint).

At the start of a sprint, the Scrum team will hold a planning session with the product owner. This session is to look at the product backlog and identify what 'chunks' will go into the sprint, and how the team will go about delivering that work. The product owner's role is to prioritise the backlog so the Scrum team is working on the highest priority features during a sprint. (Although the sprint team may digress from this a little, for example if there is a technical reason during sprint planning to complete another task first).

The key thing is that the team accepts into the sprint **only the work that they feel confident can be completed in full** so any piece of code planned for a sprint has to be written, tested and fully functional by the end of that sprint. This means that the chunks of product backlog get 'chunked down' again into smaller items of stand-alone value.

There is a strong correlation with the Kanban framework here,

> **FAIL FAST**
>
> My daughter recently spent an hour completing an on-line job application for a large organisation, entering all her employment history, explaining why she would like to do the job and so on, before she was asked 'Have you ever worked in retail before?' When she checked No, her application was auto-matically rejected and she was unable to submit it. What an idiotic waste of her time. If it were a deal breaker, why not have this as the first question and 'fail fast'?

since this approach will also limit levels of unfinished work in the system at any one time.

At the end of the sprint, a sprint review is held so the Scrum team is able to demonstrate *fully working software* to the product owner and stakeholders. This demo means that the product owner and stakeholders can give feedback which will help to deepen the team's understanding of the requirements, and make informed decisions as to what is required in the next sprint. It also enables the team to 'fail fast' if they have created something that the product owner doesn't like.

The team also hold a Retrospective at the end of each sprint to identify opportunities to improve how they work together, and whether the Scrum process itself is working well. This **Inspect and Adapt** approach is basically PDCA and is how continuous improvement is embedded in Agile working.

Note however that the term 'sprint' implies a burst of effort. In reality, a sustainable pace is really what an Agile team is after, as per the Agile Manifesto.

My husband is a cyclist, and if we go on rides together, he is always ahead and waiting for me somewhere on the route. He often chooses steep hills for us to climb up, and to begin with, I found this demoralising. But then I looked at the hill with an Agile 'Scrum' mindset.

The goal for me is improved fitness. And you don't get fitter only once you have climbed the entire hill. You get a tiny bit fitter each time you take a bit of the hill and attack it. So I would look at the hill and set myself a mini goal. I'm going to pedal as far as that tree. If it's really steep, that tree might be only 40 feet away, but I don't care. I've accomplished the goal. Now I rest for a few seconds then set a new goal. And before I know it, I'm at the top of the hill. I am breaking down the main goal into sprints and achieving continuous delivery of value in the form of a tiny level of increased fitness each time I complete one.

Notes

Scrum vs Waterfall

Scrum was developed because its founders realised that the traditional waterfall model did not work for delivery of complex software products where the end result depended upon a clear definition of what was required right at the start. Actually, this failure applies to the vast majority of major IT change projects that have taken place.

What is waterfall and why doesn't it work in these situations?

Here's a simple example. Let's say you and I want to set up an on-line holiday cottage rental company. We need a website, so we write a specification for what we want, send it off to various organisations and select the lucky provider. This is waterfall, because we are using a standard step by step process, which could be shown on a Gantt chart as a sequence of steps, with each step being completed before the next can begin:

a. Write specification for website
b. Select provider
c. Design
d. Build
e. Test

    f.   User test and sign-off

    g.   Deliver

The Gantt chart looks like a cascade of steps, or a 'waterfall' with an arrow flowing from the end of one box to the start of the next.

So we are locked into a specification early on, even though we have never done this before, and the website company designs to that original specification, and then they build it, and send us a few wireframes on a weekly basis to check in with us that all is well. It seems to be going swimmingly! Then they say they are moving into testing, which is exciting for us! Then we get to test it, and find 50 things we need to change. This of course, will cost us money unless they are 'bugs'. We get into heated debates over some fundamental features that either are missing or we didn't want, but were misinterpreted, and the build is too far along to be unpicked now. Every conversation feels like a compromise. We finally sign off as we have no more money, and accept the website delivery as we limp off into the sunset.

So Scrum was created, as a direct challenge to waterfall, and asks why does the customer have to decide early on what they want? What if instead, they just had to decide what the first few features were, and put them in order of priority? What if just the most important feature was developed in the first sprint *and built and shown to them*, and everyone learned more about the requirements from that demo? What if the website design company said that change is good, because it means our understanding of your requirements has deepened?

These are the principles of Scrum. Using the Scrum framework is how many organisations approach the core principles of Agile working, including being able to respond to changing customer requirements.

So let's look at how a website provider would have worked on our holiday cottage website using Scrum:

1. They would have helped us to prioritise the product backlog. Let's say that as the joint product owners, you and I decide that the most important items on the backlog are the ability to show available cottages to rent within a given date range, and hide those that are already booked.

2. The provider's Scrum team has accepted these 2 items into its first sprint, and has chosen a 2 week sprint length. The sprint goal is to enable the user to input a date range and execute a search, then see only which cottages match the dates. During the sprint, the Scrum team build a tiny part of the front end of the website, a small part of the database, write a small amount of code, and test that it all works.

3. This fully working software is demonstrated to us at the end of the sprint (the sprint review) and we give feedback. Since we are seeing fully functioning software, we don't need to visualise the product. What did we like, and what didn't we like? Since the Scrum team discover this from the first sprint, they 'fail fast' ie they don't waste time creating code for features that will later be rejected by us.

4. Following the sprint review, we decide the priorities for the next sprint. We would like to add in the feature of showing cottages with a flexibility of 3 days either side of the date range, and the ability to conduct a search by entering a region via a dropdown list. The team agree this as the sprint goal, plan the sprint and the sprint begins. And so on.

So feedback loops are only 2 weeks long and are based on a demo of real working software. Note that this code is *not* a proof of concept ie done for show to be properly completed later. It is live working software that will be part of the final code created. Or in Agile speak, not just done, but 'done done'.

There are huge advantages to this Scrum approach:

a. Instead of waiting for the entire product to be built, you and I could theoretically launch the website after the first few sprints and start earning income. This is how Scrum achieves continuous delivery of value, not just value right at the end upon delivery

b. We could pull the plug on the project at any time, and still have a fully functioning website that works, up to the last sprint delivery. And since the team worked in strict priority order, the most important features will already be in place

c. We are not locked into early decisions

d. Any misunderstandings are quickly corrected as they occur, so we 'fail fast'

e. Since a sprint must create a piece of working software which is built and tested in the same sprint, knowledge of the end to end process quickly builds. All the pain is felt at the front end, so it has a slow start, but this is where all the key learning is done so the team gets faster and faster afterwards, with minimal rework at the end

Compare this to our traditional 'waterfall' version, where the project was delivered for user test once all of the build was complete, and *only then* did we have a working product, or even truly understand what we had asked for. Since the specification was locked down early on, we were stuck with features we no longer wanted, and didn't think of those that should have been included. All because a Gantt chart *told us* that that is what we should do!

I highly recommend reading **'Scrum: The Art of Doing Twice the Work in Half the Time'** by Jeff Sutherland.

Vertical Slicing

To ensure they can deliver stand-alone, end to end pieces of working software at the end of each sprint, a Scrum team will often use the concept of 'vertical slicing'. Imagine a huge chocolate cake comprised of many layers. Take a vertical slice through, so you can taste all of the layers together. You don't have to eat the whole cake to know whether you like it, just a little bit of each layer.

You saw the concept of vertical slicing in the holiday cottage example. To get the first sprint, we took a slice vertically through each layer of the website (front end, database, back end) to create a small amount of fully working software that allowed the user to conduct a search. We didn't build the entire database – just a small part of it. We didn't worry about the whole presentation of the website – just one field. And we learned quickly as a result. We learned that the customer prefers dropdowns to tick boxes. We learned that there was a constraint around the number of fields in our database. We learned our testing process wasn't error proofed. We learned.

Let's apply the vertical slicing principle at home. Let's say a requirement is to redecorate the whole of the upstairs of your house. The typical waterfall approach says that you would strip wallpaper from every room, then prep every wall, then hang lining paper on every wall, and then hang your wallpaper. Classic step by step, horizontal slicing, one layer at a time. The strip layer, prep layer, line layer and wallpaper layer.

But what if you realised at the final step, that the prep hadn't been carried out very well, and you could still see all the bumps in the walls after you had hung the first piece of wallpaper? What a disaster! Your home has been in chaos for weeks, and you now have all that rework to do.

The vertical slice approach is to break down the requirement and just do *one wall* to completion. Strip, prep, line the wall then hang wallpaper on it. You have taken a thin slice through the layers. The problems with the finish are immediately spotted when you finish the wall. You deliver fast, you 'fail fast', and adapt your approach. From then on, you take a thicker slice and complete one room at a time, in order of priority. If you pull the plug on the project, you don't have a house full of chaos. You have the most important rooms completed. And you get the benefit of the improvement each time you finish a room – continuous delivery of value. With waterfall, only when you had finished the whole house would you have benefited from all your hard work.

Another example of waterfall versus vertical slicing is in house building. Imagine you are a construction company, building a fleet of swish new houses. A vertical slice would be to just build one house, complete it, identify any issues and snags, sell it, get income and then build the next. This way, you are not left with a lot of unfinished houses (wip) that take a year to complete and then go on the market together. The argument against a vertical slice approach is that it is far less efficient use of tradesmens' time to only work on one house at a time. The argument for it is the property company which is currently having to retrospectively replace fire barriers at 37% of its homes on one estate. The negative publicity associated with this – including where residents have had to move into temporary accommodation as a safety measure – cannot be costed. Had just one house been built and thoroughly checked before beginning the second, the defect would have been identified and rectified then and there for future builds.

Minimum Viable Product (MVP)

The concept of Minimum Viable Product (MVP) is often used by Agile teams when vertically slicing the work. MVP is the least amount of effort that you need to make a viable product that people will want, and has just enough features for you to gather sufficient feedback on it. In the home decorating example, the wall was enough to tell us we needed to change the process, but no one would be happy if we just finished one wall. It wasn't a viable product. So MVP in this case would be one room. In the Introduction to this book, an airport example was used to explain Agile working. MVP was the concept used when I suggest building just the key components of the airport needed to get it operational.

Note that MVP is closely related to removing the Waste of Over Production, since both seek to eliminate unnecessary work.

Here are more examples of MVP:

1. Instead of setting up a new book store, where you aren't sure what the consumer demand is, set up a pop-up shop and trial which books sell the best.
2. Instead of taking a year to write a book, write a blog. A blog is an Agile book.
3. Instead of opening a new restaurant, create a supper club and test your menus. Or a takeaway service.
4. Instead of launching a whole new hospital, just build one outpatients' clinic, one theatre and one ward. Get them each working perfectly for one specialty, apply the learning then expand quickly.
5. For local councils, instead of waiting months to close the left hand lane of a litter-strewn A road while litter pickers are safely deployed over a 10 mile stretch, just do 500 ft at a time, once per week. The dirtiest stretch first. And increase fines on littering while you are at it.
6. Instead of waiting for the entire interior of your new home to be completed before you move in, install one bathroom, one shower and the kitchen appliances. This means you can save money on renting another property at the same time as the build, and give early feedback of any issues to your builder!

Imagine Brexit had used a vertical slice approach. Imagine that we had said, Let's start with the Irish border. Or immigration. Or whatever was deemed most important. Let's just do that. And let's have European representation at each of our meetings, so we understand what will be deemed reasonable, and 'fail fast'. Let's agree and secure that piece of legislation. Now we have something that is solid, we can use our learning to do the next most important 'slice'. I believe that the overall process would have had a far greater chance of success.

An Agile world would be a huge improvement.

Notes

Lean *and* Agile

So Lean is about creating customer value and eliminating waste, while Agile is about creating customer value faster and responding to change. Both Scrum and Kanban frameworks are similar to Lean in that they improve the flow of work and actively reduce wip, and are key drivers of continuous improvement. The principles of Scrum mean that rework is reduced overall – it is greater at the beginning, but there should be no surprises upon delivery of the final product. Importantly, both Agile and Lean advocate the empowerment of teams rather than managers to take control of the work.

Given this, let's look at how Agile can best be used together with Lean to drive the best results.

Using Lean and Agile in a local improvement

Here is a simple example. Let's say that you are a junior member of the HR team and have been asked to create a general induction guide on your intranet for new starters in your organisation. You might get a group of colleagues together, agree the key subject headings, each member chooses a subject to complete, and you all meet up periodically to check progress and build the guide. Then you all review the finished ensemble to make editorial suggestions, finalise and publish.

It's a Lean improvement, right? The new starter only needs to look at this document to understand how to book meetings, what team events are on, and so forth. Previously, a new starter would have had to ask multiple people multiple questions to get this information, or search the intranet for help on each subject.

So, yes, it's a Lean improvement as it tackles the Wastes of People Movement and Waiting and Delays. But if it takes 6 weeks for the team to pull together the document, and then 1 week to be revised with all the changes, and you had 10 new starters in that time, you missed the boat. You were slow to market, so to speak. Plus the approach itself doesn't feel very Lean as there was a lot of handling of the work.

If we combine a Scrum approach with this Lean improvement, we get a far better result. In Scrum, the subject headings would have been ordered in terms of priority. What is the single most important piece of information to a new starter? Let's say they tell you it's a list of places to eat lunch. Now vertically slice using MVP. Create just one page, get a member to review it and then *publish this one page that day*. This means that within a day of starting the project, you have already created value. If a new starter arrives on day 2, they can immediately use this information. No one has to wait until your team has finished the entire document to start using it.

Feedback from your new starter provides a useful change to the formatting and he mentions it would have been helpful to know vegetarian options, and that the local café only took cash. This information improves the first page. You quickly redo the formatting and apply it to page two, which includes an organisational structure and brief company history. This is published straightaway. And so on. No Waste of Rework at the end. No Waste of Waiting and Delays while everyone composes their pieces. Instead, you Inspect and Adapt via the feedback given, and provide continuous delivery of value in priority order.

LEAN AND AGILE CAR RENTAL

A Lean and Agile approach can be applied to the airport rental car example from earlier. We have already seen how the team might set up a Kanban board to manage the work in getting the cars ready. But to truly optimise the improvement, they would have also used Lean to eliminate the waste end to end. If I were to redesign the car rental process, customers would receive a text alert or email as soon as they landed, telling them that their car was ready and waiting, showing its exact location on their phone via GPS. They can choose to have an attendant meet them at the car. The attendants can see their location, so they can manage their workload and be there to greet if necessary. Customers go straight to the parking bay, sign the contract electronically by phone, and if they don't need an attendant, are sent a code to open a box for the keys and drive away. At the barrier, they stop for 30 seconds whilst cameras take multiple photos of the car. They are on their way within 5 minutes. No need to go to the rental office at all! No paperwork! No checking for damage! Value has been made to flow by using Lean to eliminate waste, and the daily operation of preparing the car is managed via Agile using the Kanban board.

So we have a simple Lean improvement, but it uses an Agile approach to implement it. We have created customer value faster and responded quickly to changing requirements.

How would you use Agile in a full-scale Lean transformation?

Let's start with a Lean-only approach:

1. Set up the team and ensure senior leadership buy-in
2. Have a highly interactive workshop to explain value and the 7 Wastes plus 1, and the principles of Lean. (I like to use a Lego game to do this). Work with the team to map their key process end to end, showing the wasteful steps as well as the value created
3. Divide a flipchart into two columns and ask them to list all wastes from the current process in the left column. Then get them to identify any possible solutions in the right column. This means that the team is selling the change to themselves,

right from the start. Gather data around key measurements to complete the As Is picture

4. If there is a key problem to resolve that is blocking the team, use the structured problem solving wheel or Ishikawa

5. Use SECAR and other Lean tools to design a future state process map. You will have eliminated a lot of waste, reduced dependencies, embedded Poka Yoke and Quality Assurance to eliminate rework loops and challenged your Quality Control points – why are they needed, and if they are, are they early on so that we 'fail fast'?

6. Ask the team to check 90% of the wastes identified in the 3rd step will be eliminated by the new process. If yes, you have successfully identified the new way of working and addressed root causes of waste. This is a powerful moment within the team

7. Help create a visual plan as per Chapter 4 to implement the change. (I usually ask them to create a 30 day plan for quick wins, and a medium term plan for everything else. It will include communications, resourcing and training)

8. The team get agreement to proceed. Using the 30 day plan, they get the quick wins under their belt before moving onto the main plan

9. The whole process is repeated with a different key business process, and a different local team. Repeat until everyone in the organisation gets Lean and is on board. Train managers to support, encourage, facilitate and challenge. Measure and celebrate successes. Communicate the wins. Remove obstacles. Learn from the fails. And keep going.

There is nothing *fundamentally wrong* with this approach. I have had real success with it over the years! However, the following are notable:

- The Lean transformation is a waterfall approach.
- For each process, other than the quick wins, most changes are implemented between 3 and 6 months, so there is a delay before the benefits are realised. Most of the learning about how to do change is upon delivery.
- There are lots of part-finished improvement projects in play across the organisation, which can be demanding of resources, and can cause communication issues and confusion. A Lean transformation can lack momentum as a consequence. The organisation and even the steering group may struggle to maintain focus and direction as things take a long time to come to full fruition.

The Lean and Agile approach

Let's extract the key principles of Scrum and Kanban:

- take the requirements and break them down into stand-alone items of value
- always work in order of your customer's priority
- focus on continuous delivery of value
- stop starting and start finishing
- self-organised teams
- inspect and adapt
- 'fail fast'

Now look at the above Lean transformation from a Scrum viewpoint:

In effect, the steering group is playing the role of 'super' product owner. And they have broken the work down into 'chunks' – but the chunks are processes. In Scrum terms, these chunks are too big. You will not create continuous delivery of value, because you are doing a whole process change at a time.

Here's how the same transformation would be done using Lean *and* Agile:

- The steering group identify the top 5 processes they want to improve, across the organisation. There will be therefore 5 local change teams
- Each team maps their current process and uses Lean tools to identify and quantify say the 3 biggest areas of waste for each process, ie 15 in total, and any quick wins
- The list of 15 wastes is the product backlog. Note that the senior manager for each process should be part of the steering group, to bring context to each waste and explain its importance. The steering group then jointly agree the priority order of the product backlog
- The first waste is worked on with the local team to eliminate *just that waste and nothing else.* The product owner is the senior manager for that process. The team are using vertical slicing, because they are taking a slice through each of the Lean improvement steps and applying them to just one of the wastes identified.
- Next is the second highest priority issue, often within another process. And so on. So you do *not* implement all 3 changes to a process at a time, unless these have been agreed as joint priority. You just do one.
- In the meantime, nothing is stopping the local teams from putting in place the quick wins that were identified during the initial phase. Their managers should be actively supporting them in doing this
- The steering group continues to prioritise, but there are only ever a maximum of 15 items on the backlog at any time. Note that the product backlog is dynamic and evolving – the whole point of Agile is that the world changes, and we need to be responsive as

a consequence. So there is no point in prioritising all 15 issues in strict order, just the top 5.

So a Lean and Agile approach to this Lean transformation means that Lean is used to identify and eliminate the highest priority wastes, and Agile via a Scrum framework is used to manage the change, using a vertical slice approach.

It might feel that you are only part-delivering in each area, so how can you be successful? Isn't this fragmented 'pockets' of improvement?

Yes.

But you will move so fast through the organisation that instead of waiting for change to happen, people will quickly see it affect them. This is a powerful motivator to get on board. Remember that one of the most important aspects of change is engaging people. As you are always working in priority order, your improvements reap rewards faster and people (including the steering group) see the stuff that matters most gets done first. Prioritising the product backlog correctly is crucial for this reason.

How is the priority of the backlog decided? I've suggested it's the biggest area of waste currently. But instead perhaps the steering group decide that it's the best improvement to get engagement. Perhaps it's the greatest hindrance of performance. It's really down to the local teams to ensure they identify the biggest issue for them, and the steering group to make the final decision on the overall priority, and be transparent around decision making.

The 'fail fast' principle is key. Didn't communicate the change properly? Training not up to scratch? Didn't understand the constraints? You learned early from your mistakes because the change happened faster, and you applied the learning to the next change.

> The local teams can use sprints to plan and deliver the change. Where an issue is a high priority but several other things need to happen first, the steering group may decide to place these seemingly lower priority items first on the product backlog, as they are enablers to the bigger change.

AGILE IS ABOUT RESPONDING TO CHANGE

With a Lean and Agile approach to transformation, you are better able to respond to change. If the organisation suddenly needs to stop the programme or change the focus, then the most important improvements will have been done. If the feedback on how an improvement was implemented is poor, the approach can be changed very quickly. And since you are only focused on one process change at a time with a team, and there are only 15 issues at a time on the backlog, work in progress is kept low and the overall transformation is delivered faster. It also makes the plan clearer and more believable.

With a waterfall approach, you will have a large number of part-finished improvements in place, making it more difficult to respond quickly to change, and the transformation happens at a far slower pace because you are batching the improvements rather than slicing them.

Examples of Lean and Agile

Example 1 – The publishing company

I worked with a large publisher a few years ago to help them implement some Lean improvements, working with 4 separate teams on 4 different business processes. We used all of the Lean tools described in this book to make the changes. They had a very strong Learning and Development manager and she just got it. The senior leadership team was so smitten with what these teams achieved in terms of process improvements that they decided to implement Lean across the whole organisation, and seconded a team of 14 internal change agents full-time for 12 months to help them do it.

An amazing commitment to Lean. I trained the change agents, left them to it, and in the meantime, discovered Agile.

A few months later, I returned to the publishing client to see how the change agents had been getting on.

They had a problem. Change was happening far too slowly, so the business was losing heart – each change agent had taken an area and had worked with the local team to map all the processes, and identify all the waste in that area. Then they had drawn up a plan to deliver the new Lean process in that area as a 'Big Bang'.

But the process was taking months and nothing had yet been delivered. There was a lot of documentation that seemed to need updating, and lots of meetings to discuss all of the changes. People were getting bored waiting for change to happen. Worse, the analytical work everyone was putting into identifying the waste would be out of date by the time they actually made the improvements.

They were batching the change.

And one of their biggest delays to implementation was the training team – there weren't enough of them available to train teams in how to work the new processes.

> I recently attended a forum hosted by a provider who was working across 15 NHS trusts. This provider had delivered an electronic document management system to everyone there, and there was one key area of value that all the trusts had agreed should be developed as a priority as it would remove a great deal of waste for the admin teams at each trust.
>
> To the group's chagrin, the provider revealed that the delivery date had slipped for this functionality, because they were also going to incorporate a number of other features at the same time. None of these other features was a priority by comparison. Had they just focused on delivering the one item that really added value, rather than batching the change, they would not have had to slip the due date by 4 months and infuriate their customers.

Breakthrough. This is when I first realised that Agile working does not just apply to software development companies!

I suggested using a Scrum approach to their Lean change. As in the previous example, each change agent would just do *one improvement at a time, in priority order.* Whatever was delivered had to work as a stand-alone piece of value. For example, let's say the biggest problem with the production department was a particular machine always breaking down. Replacing the most frequently failing part for that machine would be the highest priority for the change team. By making only that change, the machine was down

EXAMPLE 2 – THE AGILE HOSPITAL ■ 117

for only 2 hours (had all the machine improvements been made together, they would have waited weeks for a big chunk of planned downtime). The improvement to the dept would be felt immediately.

Because the changes were smaller, the trainers could run a 60 minute training session rather than a 1 day workshop. Bingo – trainers were no longer a bottleneck. Documentation was kept short and simple in line with MVP. Most importantly, the timescales to actually achieving the next improvement would reduce from 7 months to a few weeks, so the pace of change would increase.

If any part of the change process itself didn't work well, such as communicating the change, then the team had much faster feedback and could adjust accordingly next time using Inspect and Adapt.

Most importantly, people could see value being delivered and would engage in the change!

Example 2 – The Agile hospital

I was working with an extremely competent operations director of a foundation trust hospital, and she was responsible for the build and delivery of a new £100m hospital being built on the site over the next 3 years. She asked my thoughts on a possible approach to getting the operational side of the hospital ready in time.

She had an excellent senior team in place, but my concern was that the approach they were considering was to set up separate workstreams for IT, admin, outpatients, inpatients, medical records and so on. Each of these workstreams would be tasked with getting their operational processes ready, using the new layout plans provided. All of the teams' outputs would then come together to build a final solution for the operation.

My concern was that the separate workstream approach simply wouldn't work, because each team would make assumptions and decisions that would affect the other teams. Unless each team had a representative attending all meetings, which would be hugely wasteful, there could well be a tremendous amount of rework involved when issues came to light down the line. For example, imagine that the admin workstream designed the operational process for outpatients, and while this was shared with everyone, the subtleties escaped IT who only later realised they were unable to provide the network ports for that particular layout in reception. IT had not been part of that workstream and so had not picked up on certain nuances and constraints. No one would know until it was too late, so the entire reception layout would have to be reconfigured with a knock-on impact on the outpatient process, and so on.

I explained to the team the concept of Agile and vertical slicing, and suggested that we should use this approach instead. Instead of horizontally slicing the programme into separate functions, as they had suggested, we would vertically slice by service, with all functions represented in each 'layer'.

So we would take a service (for example outpatient clinics), and define how it would work, using IT, admin, ops management, outpatients, inpatients and medical records to jointly agree the process and layout. Then we would apply the learning to the next service, and so on.

We got a big team together, including nurses, medical doctors and surgeons, and explained Agile working. We asked them to identify and prioritise for us the first vertical slice for the hospital. They chose Urology Outpatients, because this service would have so many touchpoints with other departments within the process. The next step was to have a workshop involving everyone so that we could agree the current state process for Urology Outpatients and define the future state. We overlaid the new process with the build layout and checked that the new process could be achieved.

One interesting outcome from the first workshop was the realisation that there were no patient changing rooms in the designated Outpatients area. This would have slowed down the examinations because the

EXAMPLE 3 – THE MARKETING CAMPAIGN ■ 119

consultant couldn't see the next patient until their current patient was dressed. We failed fast, so could adapt quickly.

I warned it would take a few months to do the first one or two service designs, and then afterwards it would go faster, because the constraints and the best ways forward would already be known. They would also get a deeper understanding of the requirements, and the level of detail needed. And they would deliver a much better hospital as a result.

One of the biggest things you will need to overcome with Agile is our ingrained tendency to use waterfall! We are so used to doing things step by step that it feels strange to slice through the steps. And even though the hospital team totally understood the principle of vertical slicing, most of them assumed that we would start the next slice with the operational processes on paper only. And then deliver all services in one go when the hospital opened its doors.

I call this the waterfall trap. It's only Agile if you take the slice all the way through to delivery, since only this is continuous delivery of value. There was no reason why they couldn't start delivering each newly designed service in their *existing hospital* as each slice was completed. It would be the best way to Inspect and Adapt. And it makes change far easier if people are simply copying across what they have already become accustomed to doing when the new hospital opens.

Example 3 – The marketing campaign

A friend of mine was working with a marketing team which had a number of issues. The company had a number of small teams located across the UK, each with marketing personnel in them, and there was also a centralised marketing department based in London. Each local team created different content for the company's campaigns with no overall content owner, so the branding was muddled, and there was no transparency in terms of what different teams were doing, leading to duplicated or inconsistent content with each team.

Her starting point was to get together all of the teams, identify the wastes with the current state process and agree just 3 things they would change. They then trialled these changes and reviewed how much things had improved. One of these improvements was to use a steering group to set the campaigns in an overall priority order that they would all follow. Another improvement was to ensure a dedicated product owner for the content of the first big campaign, using a Scrum framework.

Interestingly, the team had in mind that they would launch the campaign in 2020, but my friend in her capacity as Scrum master coached them in continuous delivery of value. They broke down the campaign into chunks of stand-alone value. And from the first few sprints the team started to deliver 'shippable content' of marketing material that the product owner was happy to approve the use of.

So the starting point was to use a Lean methodology to challenge the waste in the current ways of working. This was followed by trialling just a few new ways of working, and breaking down and prioritising the work to deliver it faster via a Scrum framework.

Example 4 – The energy consultancy

An energy consultant friend specialises in reducing energy costs for pharmaceutical companies world-wide. One of his frustrations is that despite being able to prove that his company can reduce their bills by millions of pounds, some of his clients still take a long time to schedule in the work. This is particularly prevalent with very large organisations, where literally hundreds of initiatives are jostling for place and the leadership teams seem to find it hard to make decisions as to which to do first.

My suggestion was that he encourage his clients to create a list of all their current initiatives (each a major project in its own right) and just prioritise the top 10. He commented that just doing this would be a great step forward, even if they never did any of his projects! I encouraged him to work with his client's leadership team and for each initiative, strip out the

EXAMPLE 4 – THE ENERGY CONSULTANCY ■ 121

most important deliverable. What they needed was a product backlog of *components* of these initiatives that would make the biggest difference. This would prevent the company from working a whole initiative at a time, and since the changes were smaller the work would move faster and the 10 most important items would be completed. They would then 'pull' the next 10 items and so on.

> **USING LEAN AND AGILE TOGETHER**
>
> I promise you, if you use a Lean and Agile approach, you will start delivering change faster, your change program will be energised, mistakes quickly learned from, and your people engaged from the start because they are trusted to own the process and identify the most important changes first.

His energy savings project would be no different. His team had already worked with the client to identify where the energy savings were the biggest across all sites globally. The difference was that they now needed to break these projects down into just the most important stand-alone components. These improvements would go on the overall product backlog and be prioritised by the leadership team along with everything else.

The leadership team's role would be to maintain momentum by continuing to keep the top items on the product backlog in priority order. I suggested that a change team could be set up to engage with local teams and produce the list of initiatives at the right size of work for the leadership team to prioritise (my friend would continue to do this for the energy saving projects). As each initiative came up, the relevant front line team would be coached by the change team in using either Kanban boards or sprints to manage the change.

Rather than the Waste of Waiting and Delays, the most important initiatives would always be moving forwards and be implemented fast, creating continuous delivery of value.

Notes

Myths and Pitfalls

There is an awful lot of misinformation out there. Here are some of my most common sightings:

1. We want to 'Lean' the organisation, meaning reduce headcount. (Bad choice of words, and nothing whatsoever to do with Lean)
2. Lean is about doing things faster. (Sometimes it's about slowing things down at the front end so value flows faster downstream. You separate out your cutlery in the drawer so that you can lay the table faster later on)
3. 5 S is the 'fluffy stuff' – it doesn't deliver real change. (It's a key foundation of Lean)
4. We *are* Agile, we do daily stand-ups. (I don't know where to start with this one)
5. Agile is just about Plan Do Check Act. (That's a tiny part of it, yes)
6. We are sprinting. (Actually all you are doing is breaking down the work into things called Sprint 1, Sprint 2 etc. There is no concept of continuous delivery of value, or stand-alone items of value, or completing all aspects of the work within a sprint, or not locking down requirements early. Sprinting is only one way

of approaching Agile working, but don't kid yourself you are sprinting when you're not)

7. This is my Kanban board. (No wip limits, so no pull, so just a tracking board then)

8. Sprint planning sessions and sprint reviews are a nuisance for the customer (if the product owner doesn't have time to come to these meetings, then they don't want the product enough. Solution – move the team to another project or change the product owner to someone who is going to invest their time in getting it right)

9. I manage an Agile team (Agile teams are self-organising so they don't need managing)

10. Agile means breaking down the work and doing it in priority order using sprints. (Incorrect. The Agile Manifesto says nothing at all about doing this. It also says nothing at all about sprinting. Scrum is simply *one* of the frameworks that is used by organisations to achieve Agile working. The *Scrum approach to Agile working* is to break down the work and deliver in priority order, using sprints. It's an important distinction. It is perfectly possible to be an Agile organisation and have never used sprints or a product backlog)

11. We are Agile! We are making the plan up as we go along! (Inspect and Adapt, yes. But let's be careful here, or anyone without a plan could badge themselves as Agile, when in truth they could just be incompetent).

Sustaining the Change

Improvements only count if they are sustained.

A Lean and Agile transformation is a very big change for your organisation. Combining the two approaches gives you the optimum way to succeed, but remember that it is all about people. If you want to keep the benefits of a big change over the long term, the context around the change is crucial. How receptive is the culture to change? Are there a number of people things (outlined in this book) that you need to start working on first? This helps to create the right environment for transformational change to succeed.

Often I advise an organisation to build competency in their managers and teams before they try to be Lean. And although the transformation must be led from the top, organisations should also start fostering a ground-up culture of continuous improvement, as with the Toyota Production System model. Managers need to listen to their teams' ideas and help facilitate the improvements that *they* come up with. The term I like is 'listening with fascination'. It means really listening to people, rather than listening on the surface whilst simply waiting to break in with your own thoughts. This is something that every manager should practice – it is a real skill. How many 1 to 1 sessions have you cancelled? How much of the time are you speaking rather than listening – this is *their* time with *you.*

(By the way, the other 2 attributes that a manager must have are courage and empathy. The courage to have difficult conversations and not hide behind emails when you are managing people. And a manager who has no empathy for their team members has no business being a manager. When I went through a close family bereavement, my interim manager texted me every day to check that I was okay, and told me not to worry about work, that I needed to focus on being with family. My 'real' manager came back from leave and replied, 'Oh' when I mentioned that I had recently been bereaved, never once asked me how I was, never mentioned the subject again and quoted the company rulebook when I wanted to take 3 weeks paid leave. Which of these managers do you think I would have walked to the end of the earth for?)

Far better to move your organisation into a better starting position first, rather than throwing massive change at people without them being ready. I deeply believe that a Lean and Agile transformation delivers huge benefits when done well, but the whole approach has to be right.

When I talk to organisations who have tried to implement any kind of significant change programmes, I draw the picture below and ask if it resonates with what they were trying to achieve:

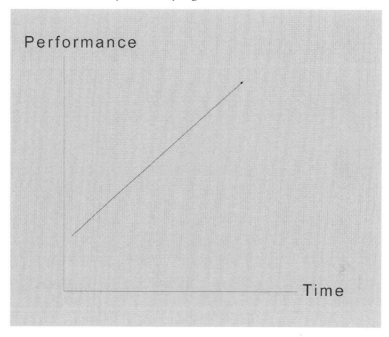

They all agree. Improved performance over time with a nice steep gradient; who wouldn't want that?

Then I overlay the graph with change cycles. It shows a company trying to achieve performance improvement via a series of big changes, one after the other. Change, change, change as below:

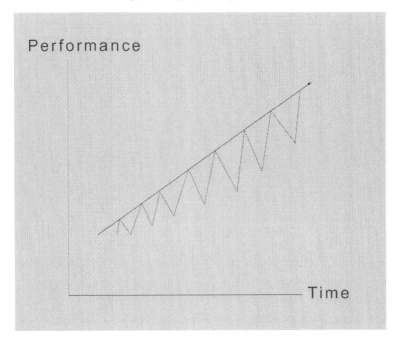

Again, this often resonates.

'How would this kind of change make you feel?' I ask them.

'Exhausted, confused, resentful,' is a common response from front line teams (note – not senior teams). When I ask whether this type of change has ever happened in their organisation, they often answer, 'This is *always* how change happens here!'

A misguided concept is that the fastest route to transformation is to follow change with change. The problem is, the above graph only plays to the 'stars' in that organisation. The elite few who were part of the change process and helped drive the improvements. However, a change will die on its feet if the vast majority of those working the process have not engaged with the change, or are too exhausted to do so. I am not saying that every person will deliberately seek to dismantle and undermine the new ways of working. But when you are tired of having big changes forced on you, you try to find ways to go back to how things used to be done so that your life can be simple again. This is the comfort food of an organisation.

Here is the *reality* of the above graph:

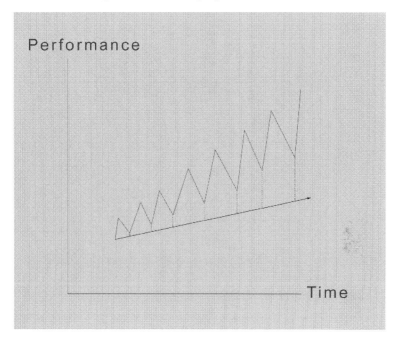

You can see that the *real* performance improvement has a much smaller gradient. And just think of all the work that went into these change cycles! People have expended huge amounts of effort, for relatively small gains. Often with this approach, the transformation happens, but it doesn't deliver the benefits it promised, and any improvements it did achieve are often not sustained as performance trickles backwards over time. Just like the red dotted lines on this graph.

Here is my recommended route to success:

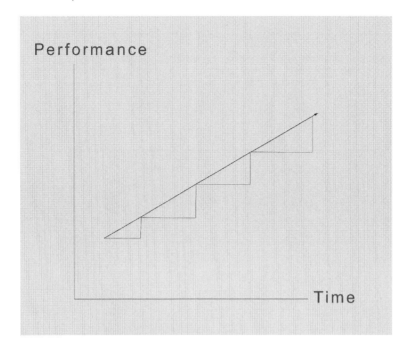

This graph doesn't play to the star players, it plays to everyone. Continuous improvement. Make a change, stabilise the change, learn from it, then continue. As long as you are doing the changes in the right priority order, this will work so much better.

In the Lean and Agile approach to transformation, generally only one change was done at a time to each key process. This gives breathing space each time. So another way to prioritise the backlog is to understand whether continuing with the next biggest issue for a process is going to lead to change fatigue for that team, and adjust the priority order accordingly.

Global companies are even more at risk of project overload, because it can be very difficult to identify all of the projects in play at any one time. Additionally, pet projects often require resource from lots more people than leaders realise, including stretched resources that underpin the daily operation. These requirements fly under the radar so that senior teams do not understand the burden they are placing on people who are already trying to deliver on a daily basis, and are taken by surprise when quality goes downhill. No one can do it all.

Of course, transformational change can be a vital requirement. Your company may need to completely restructure, or change its business model, or the way it operates. External factors such as new regulations or legal changes or technological advances can create the drive for this. Sometimes there is no option but to go for the 'Big Bang' – although you should always challenge whether these huge changes could be vertically sliced into more manageable chunks of stand-alone rather than done all at once. You can still follow the final graph above if you use this method. Embed and standardise each change so that there is a solid platform to keep building on.

You might argue that market forces don't give you enough time to do this. I would ask you, do you want to do change fast, or do you want to do it right?

Remember, change is painful. It actually registers as pain in the brain. You don't perform surgery on someone and ask them back in for a new operation the following week.

Count how many pet projects there are right now in your organisation. I once helped a company with just 250 employees, and we counted 54 active projects that people were working on – as well as their day jobs! Some years ago when I worked as a consultant at a health care trust, the CEO told me that she had almost 200 objectives to deliver across her senior management team within the next 2 years. When we reviewed them, it was because with changing NHS policies, new objectives were continually added, but no one had removed the old ones.

A lot of these objectives had been started but had stalled, so there was a lot of part-finished work everywhere but not much actual value had been delivered. This, despite a huge emphasis on Gantt charts and project managers! I advised her to pick the top 5 objectives and just focus on delivering them before anything else. Had I known about Scrum at the time, we could have looked at vertically slicing the objectives to create a product backlog of the most important components of each. We could also have considered getting her teams to set up sprints or Kanban boards to deliver the work.

Implementing Lean and Agile even as a vertical slice approach doesn't fully protect your organisation from feeling this pain. It is still transformational change. Creating the competencies and environment for change first will certainly help, but change is still hard. The pace with which you introduce it is extremely important. Let people come to terms with the change each time you do a new one.

Inspect and Adapt. Be responsive to the changing needs of the people undergoing the process.

Better to make a 20% improvement that sticks, than an 80% improvement that never really takes root and confuses and disengages everybody.

Better to climb a peak and take people with you, than scale a mountain on your own, look behind you and find that there's no one there at all.

Acknowledgements

I am lucky in that there have been a huge number of people who have had a positive influence on my career. I cannot possibly thank them all. The following are those that I admire the most for their leadership and being supremely good at their jobs: Reg Rumble and Keith Robinson from C F Taylor; Gary Pargeter from Project 7; Richard Jones, Nigel Holness, John Healy, Ian Williamson and Stuart Meek from London Underground; Neil Stutchbury, Peter Sinden and Jennifer Neil from NHS Improvement; Jo Hunter from Frimley Health Foundation Trust.

The following have given me fantastic opportunities by taking a chance on me: Jo Westfoot and Adrian Osborne of Britax Aircraft Cabin Interiors; Simon Roberts and Tom Morgan at McLaren Racing Ltd; Carla Warnes and Annie Pearson at the Manufacturing Advisory Service; Linda Beaver at Oxford University Press.

In 2000 I became a Fellow of Manufacturing Management at Cranfield University. I'd like to take this opportunity to thank the rest of FMM59 for one of the best times of my life, in particular, Mike Dibble and Paul Dennis.

In being a superb mentor on problem solving and life in general, John Kasprowicz has had a profound effect on me and I am so lucky to have worked with him, and Nicky Bhambra also. For being fabulous work colleagues, Cath Abrams, Stacey Sampson, Shveta Kanwar, Tolu Awofisayo, Sally McGuire, Susan Abidakun, Gabriel Menkiti, Jacqueline (Jax) Parker,

Leah Adamson, Tina Southby, Ahmed Ali, Neil Barber, Julie Kerr and Dr Susie Woodrow.

To Barnaby Golden, the best Agile coach anyone could wish for. Thank you to you and Susan Abidakun for your help and advice in writing this book. Thanks also to Ali Wylie and Emma Goodwin for their creative designs for this book, in particular Ali for her beautiful artwork on the cover.

Thanks also to my children, Helena and Jamie. Helena for your practical advice, and Jamie for telling me it would never sell and keeping me grounded! To my mum also, for your encouragement. And most of all, thank you to my husband Keith Beattie. Without your help and support, this book would not have been possible.